DICTIONARY OF
GRAMMAR

DICTIONARY OF GRAMMAR

Bloomsbury Books
London

This edition published 1995 by Bloomsbury Books,
an imprint of Godfrey Cave Associates,
42 Bloomsbury Street, London, WC1B 3QJ.

ISBN 1 85471 530 5

Printed in UK

Contents

A

a *see* **indefinite article**.

a-, an- is a prefix derived from Greek, meaning 'not', 'without'. Older words using it include agnostic, anarchy, anonymous. Several modern words have been formed using it, as in apolitical, asexual, atypical.

abbreviations are shortened forms of words usually used as a space-saving technique and becoming increasingly common in modern usage. They cause problems with regard to punctuation. The common question asked is whether the letters of an abbreviation should be separated by full stops. In modern usage the tendency is to omit full stops from abbreviations. This is most true of abbreviations involving initial capital letters, as in TUC, BBC, EEC and USA. In such cases full stops should definitely not be used if one or some of the initial letters do not belong to a full word. Thus television is abbreviated to TV and educationally subnormal to ESN.

There are usually no full stops in abbreviations involving the first and last letters of a word (contractions) Dr, Mr, Rd, St, but this is a matter of taste.

Abbreviations involving the first few letters of a word, as in 'Prof' (Professor) are the most likely to have full

7

stops, as in 'Feb.' (February) but again this is now a matter of taste.

These are mostly formed by adding lower-case *s*, as in Drs, JPs, TVs. Note the absence of apostrophes. *See also* ACRONYMS.

ablative refers to a case in Latin grammar that expressed 'by, with or from'. In English this case does not exist, prepositional phrases being used its place.

-able is a suffix meaning 'that can be', as in laughable, readable, washable. *See* **adjective**.

abstract noun is a noun which is the name of a thing that cannot be touched but refers to a quality, concept or idea. Examples of abstract nouns include 'anger', 'beauty', 'courage', 'Christianity', 'danger', 'fear', 'greed', 'hospitality', 'ignorance', 'jealousy', 'kudos', 'loyalty', 'Marxism', 'need', 'obstinacy', 'pain', 'quality', 'resistance', 'safety', 'truth', 'unworthiness', 'vanity', 'wisdom', 'xenophobia', 'youth', 'zeal'. *See also* CONCRETE NOUN.

accent commonly refers to a regional or individual way of speaking or pronouncing words, as in 'a Glasgow accent'. The word is also used to mean emphasis as in 'In hotel the accent is on the second syllable of the word' or 'In fashion this year the accent is on longer skirts'.

Accent also refers to certain symbols used on some foreign words adopted into English. In modern usage, which has a tendency to punctuate less than formerly was the case, accents are frequently omitted. For example an actor's part in a play is now usually spelt role but originally it was spelt rôle, the accent on *o* being called a circumflex. The accent is most likely to be retained if it affects the pronunciation. Thus cliché and divorcé usually retain the acute accent, as it is called, on the *e*. On the other hand, the accent known as the cedilla is frequently omitted from beneath the *c* in words such as façade/facade, although it is there to indicate that the *c* is soft, pronounced like an *s*, rather than a hard sound, pronounced like a *k*. The grave accent is retained in English in some words and phrases derived from French, as *mise en scène*.

accusative refers to a case in Latin grammar, the equivalent of 'objective'. It is sometimes used in English instead of 'objective'.

acronyms, like some **abbreviations**, are formed from the initial letters of several words. Unlike abbreviations, however, **acronyms** are pronounced as words rather than as just a series of letters. For example, OPEC (Organization of Petroleum Producing Countries) is pronounced o-pek and is thus an acronym, unlike USA (United States of America) which is pronounced as a series of letters and not as a word (oo-sa or yoo-sa) and is thus an abbreviation.

Acronyms are written without full stops, as in UNESCO (United Nations Educational, Scientific and Cultural Organization). Mostly **acronyms** are written in capital letters, as in NASA (National Aeronautics and Space Administration). However, very common **acronyms**, such as Aids (Acquired Immune Deficiency Syndrome), are written with just an initial capital, the rest of the letters being lower case.

Acronyms which refer to a piece of scientific or technical equipment are written like ordinary words in lower-case letters as laser (light amplification by simulated emission of radiation.

active voice is one of two voices that verbs are divided into, the other being PASSIVE VOICE. In verbs in the active voice, commonly called *active verbs*, the subject of the verb performs the action described by the verb. Thus, in the sentence 'The boy threw the ball', 'throw' is in the active voice since the subject of the verb (the boy) is doing the throwing. Similarly, in the sentence 'Her mother was driving the car', 'driving' is in the active voice since it is the subject of the sentence (her mother) that is doing the driving. Similarly, in the sentence 'We saw the cows in the field', 'saw' is the active voice since it is the subject of the sentence (we) that is doing the seeing. *See also* PASSIVE VOICE.

acute accent refers to a mark placed over some letters in certain languages, such as French, to indicate vowel length, vowel quality, pronunciation, etc. It is found in English in some words that have been borrowed from the French, as in 'fiancé' and 'divorcé' to indicate pronunciation.

-ade is a suffix meaning 'fruit drink', as in 'lemonade', 'orangeade'.

adjectival clause is a kind of subordinate clause which describes or modifies a noun or pronoun. *See under* RELA-

TIVE CLAUSE, the name by which it is better known.

adjective is a word that describes or gives information about a noun or pronoun. It is said to qualify a noun or pronoun since it limits the word it describes in some way, by making it more specific. Thus, adding the adjective 'red' to 'book' limits 'book', since it means we can forget about books of any other colour. Similarly, adding 'large' to 'book' limits it, since it means we can forget about books of any other size.

Adjectives tell us something about the colour, size, number, quality, or classification of a noun or pronoun, as in 'purple curtains', 'jet-black hair', 'bluish eyes'; 'tiny baby', 'large houses', 'biggish gardens', 'massive estates'; five children', 'twenty questions', 'seventy-five books'; 'sad people', 'joyful occasions', 'delicious food', 'civil engineering', 'nuclear physics', 'modern languages', 'Elizabethan drama'.

Several adjectives may modify one noun or pronoun, as in 'the small, black cat', 'an enormous, red-brick, Victorian house'. The order in which they appear is flexible and can vary according to the emphasis one wishes to place on the various adjectives. However, a common sequence is size, quality, colour and classification, as in 'a small, beautiful, pink wild rose' and 'a large, ugly, grey office building'.

Adjectives do not change their form. They remain the same whether the noun to which they refer is singular or plural, or masculine or feminine.

All the above examples of adjectives come before the

noun, but not all adjectives do so. For information on
the position of adjectives *see* ATTRIBUTIVE ADJECTIVE, PREDI-
CATIVE ADJECTIVE, POST-MODIFIER.

Many **adjectives** are formed from either the past participles of verbs, and so end in *-ed*, or from the present
participles and so end in *-ing*. Examples of adjectives
ending in *-ed* include 'annoyed', 'blackened', 'coloured',
'damaged', 'escaped', 'fallen', 'guarded', 'heated',
'identified', 'jailed', 'knotted', 'labelled', 'mixed', 'numbered', 'opened', 'pleated', 'recorded', 'satisfied',
'taped', 'used', 'varied', 'walled', 'zoned'. Examples of
adjectives ending in *-ing* include 'amusing', 'boring',
'captivating', 'demanding', 'enchanting', 'fading', 'grat-
ing', 'horrifying', 'identifying', 'jarring', 'kneeling', 'la-
bouring', 'manufacturing', 'nursing', 'operating', 'part-
ing', 'quivering', 'racing', 'satisfying', 'telling', 'under-
mining', 'worrying', 'yielding'.

Several **adjectives** end in *-ical* and are formed by adding *-al* to certain nouns ending in *-ic*. Examples include
'arithmetical', 'comical', 'critical', 'cynical', 'fanatical',
'logical', 'magical', 'musical', 'mystical' and 'scepti-
cal'. Sometimes the adjectives ending in *-ical* are formed
from nouns that end in *-ics*. These include 'acoustical',
'ethical', 'hysterical', 'statistical' and 'tropical'. Several
adjectives end in *-ic* and are formed from nouns ending
in *-ics*. These include 'acoustic', 'acrobatic', 'aerobic',
'athletic', 'economic', 'electronic', 'genetic', 'gymnas-
tic', 'histrionic' and 'linguistic'.

Other common adjectival endings include *-ful*, as in

'beautiful', 'dreadful', 'eventful', 'graceful', 'hateful', 'tearful' and 'youthful'. They also include *-less*, as in 'clueless', 'graceless', 'hatless', 'meaningless' and 'sunless'.

Many adjectives end in *-able* and many end in *-ible*. There are often spelling problems with such adjectives. The following adjectives are likely to be misspelt: Some adjectives in *-able*:

abominable	definable	impeccable
acceptable	delectable	implacable
adaptable	demonstrable	impracticable
adorable	dependable	impressionable
advisable	desirable	indescribable
agreeable	discreditable	indispensable
amiable	disreputable	inimitable
approachable	durable	insufferable
available	durable	lamentable
bearable	enviable	manageable
bearable	excitable	measurable
beatable	excusable	memorable
believable	expendable	nameable
blameable	foreseeable	non-flammable
calculable	forgettable	objectionable
capable	forgivable	operable
changeable	healable	palpable
comfortable	hearable	pleasurable
commendable	immovable	preferable
conceivable	impassable	readable

Adjectives ending in *-able*:

recognizable	tenable	variable
regrettable	tolerable	viable
renewable	transferable	washable
reputable	understandable	wearable
sizeable	unmistakable	winnable
stoppable	usable	workable

Some adjectives ending in *-ible*:

accessible	divisible	perceptible
admissible	edible	permissible
audible	exhaustible	possible
collapsible	expressible	repressible
combustible	fallible	reproducible
compatible	feasible	resistible
comprehensible	flexible	responsible
contemptible	forcible	reversible
credible	gullible	risible
defensible	indelible	sensible
destructible	intelligible	susceptible
digestible	irascible	tangible
discernible	negligible	visible

See also COMPARISON OF ADJECTIVES, COMPOUNDS, DEMON-STRATIVE ADJECTIVE, DETERMINER, INTERROGATIVE ADJECTIVE and POSSESSIVE ADJECTIVE.

adverb is a word that adds to our information about a verb, as in 'work rapidly'; about an adjective, as in 'an extremely beautiful young woman'; or about another ad-

14

verb, as in 'sleeping very soundly'. **Adverbs** are said to modify the words to which they apply since they limit the words in some way and make them more specific. Thus, adding 'slowly' to 'walk', as in 'They walked slowly down the hill', limits the verb 'walk' since all other forms of 'walk', such as 'quickly', 'lazily', etc, have been discarded.

There are several different kinds of **adverbs**, categorized according to the information they provide about the word they modify. They include adverbs of time, adverbs of place, adverbs of manner, adverbs of degree, adverbs of frequency, adverbs of probability, adverbs of duration, and interrogative adverbs.

Adverbs of time tell us when something happened and include such words as 'now', 'then', 'later', 'soon', 'afterwards', 'yesterday', etc, as in 'He is due to arrive now', 'I will call you later', 'She had a rest and went out afterwards', 'They left yesterday'.

Adverbs of place tell us where something happened and include such words as 'there', 'here', 'somewhere', 'anywhere', 'thereabouts', 'abroad', 'outdoors', 'overhead', 'underground', 'hither and thither', etc, as in 'I haven't been there', 'They couldn't see her anywhere', 'His family live abroad', and 'We heard a noise overhead'.

Adverbs of manner tell us how something happens and include a wide range of possibilities. Frequently adverbs in this category are formed by adding -ly to an adjective. Examples of these include:

adjective	adverb	adjective	adverb
anxious	anxiously	mean	meanly
bad	badly	narrow	narrowly
cautious	cautiously	pale	palely
dumb	dumbly	quick	quickly
elegant	elegantly	soothing	soothingly
fearless	fearlessly	tough	toughly
hot	hotly	unwilling	unwillingly
interested	interestedly	vain	vainly
joking	jokingly	weak	weakly
lame	lamely		

Some adjectives have to be modified in some way before the suffix *-ly* is added to form the adverbs. For example, in adjectives ending in *-y*, the *y* changes to *i* before *-ly* is added. Examples of these include:

adjective	adverb	adjective	adverb
angry	angrily	happy	happily
busy	busily	merry	merrily
canny	cannily	pretty	prettily
dry	drily	silly	sillily
easy	easily	tatty	tattily
funny	funnily	weary	wearily

Note the exceptions 'shyly', 'slyly', 'wryly'.
Adjectives ending in *-e* frequently drop the *e* before adding *-ly*. Examples of these include:

adjective	adverb	adjective	adverb
able	ably	peaceable	peaceably
feeble	feebly	true	truly
gentle	gently	unintelligible	unintelligibly

Suffixes other than -*ly* that may be added to adjectives to form **adverbs of manner** include -*wards*, as in 'backwards', 'heavenwards'; -*ways*, as in 'edgeways', 'sideways'; *wise*, as in 'clockwise', 'moneywise'.

Some **adverbs of manner** may take the same form as the adjectives to which they correspond. These include 'fast', 'hard', 'solo', 'straight', 'wrong', as in 'She took the wrong book' and 'Don't get me wrong'.

Adverbs of degree tells us the degree, extent or intensity of something that happens and include 'hugely', 'immensely', 'moderately', 'adequately', 'greatly', 'strongly', 'tremendously', 'profoundly', 'totally', 'entirely', 'perfectly', 'partially', 'practically', 'virtually', 'almost', as in 'They enjoyed the show hugely', 'The office was not adequately equipped', 'We strongly disapprove of such behaviour', 'He was totally unaware of the facts', 'They are virtually penniless'.

Adverbs of frequency are used to tell us how often something happens and include 'never', 'rarely', 'seldom', 'infrequently', 'occasionally', 'periodically', 'intermittently', 'sometimes', 'often', 'frequently', 'regularly', 'normally', 'always', 'constantly', 'continually', as in 'She never eats breakfast', 'We go to the cinema occasionally', 'He goes to the dentist regularly', 'Normally they travel by bus', 'He is in pain constantly'.

Adverbs of probability tells us how often something happens and include 'probably', 'possibly', 'conceivably', 'perhaps', 'maybe', 'presumably', 'hopefully', 'definitely', 'certainly', 'indubitably', 'doubtless', as in 'You will probably see them there', 'He may conceivably pass the exam this time', 'Presumably they know that she is leaving', 'Hopefully the news will be good', 'I am definitely not going', 'He is indubitably a criminal'.

Adverbs of duration tell us how long something takes or lasts and include 'briefly', 'temporarily', 'long', 'indefinitely', 'always', 'permanently', 'forever', as in 'We stopped briefly for coffee', 'Have you known her long?', 'Her face is permanently disfigured', 'They have parted forever'.

Adverbs of emphasis add emphasis to the action described by the verb and include 'absolutely', 'certainly', 'positively', 'quite', 'really', 'simply', 'just', as in 'They absolutely detest each other', 'He positively adores her', 'She really wants to be forgiven', 'I simply must go now'

Interrogative adverbs ask questions and include 'where', 'when', 'how', and 'why', as in 'Where are you going?', 'When will you be back?', 'How will you get there?', 'Why have they asked you to go?' They are placed at the beginning of sentences, and such sentences always end with a question mark.

adverbial clauses are subordinate clauses that modify the main or principal clause by adding information about time, place, concession, condition, manner, purpose and result. They usually follow the main clause but most of them can be put in front of the main clause for reason of emphasis or style.

Adverbial clauses of time indicate the time of an event and are introduced by conjunctions such as 'after', 'as', 'as soon as', 'before', 'once', 'since', 'the minute', 'the moment', 'till', 'until', 'when', 'whenever, while', 'whilst', as in 'He left after the meal was over', 'She arrived as I was leaving', 'Once I recognized him I spoke to him', 'I recognized him the minute I saw him', 'We won't know until tomorrow' and 'The thief ran away when he saw the police'.

Adverbial clauses of place indicate the location of an event and are introduced by conjunctions such as 'where', 'wherever' or 'everywhere', as in 'He was miserable where he was', 'They left it where they found it', 'Wherever I went I saw signs of poverty' and 'Everywhere she goes she causes trouble'.

Adverbial clauses of concession contain a fact that contrasts in some way with the main clause and are introduced by conjunctions such as 'although', 'even though', 'though', 'whereas', 'while', 'whilst', as in 'I have to admire his speech, although I disagree with what he said', 'He does his best at school work even though he is not very good at it' and 'Whilst I myself do not like him I can understand why he is popular'.

Adverbial clauses of condition deal with possible situations and are introduced by the conjunctions 'if', 'only if', 'unless', 'as long as', 'providing', 'provided', as in 'If you had kept quiet they would not have known about the event', 'We cannot go unless we get permission', 'They can leave only if they have finished their work' and 'Provided he is feeling better he can leave hospital'. Inversion can be used in such clauses instead of a conjunction, as in 'Had you been present you would have been most amused' and 'Had he any sense he would leave now'.

Adverbial clauses of manner describe the way that someone behaves or the way in which something is done, and are introduced by conjunctions such as 'as', 'as if', 'as though', 'like', 'the way', as in 'Why does he behave as he does', 'He slurred his speech as though he were drunk' and 'He looked at her as if he hated her'.

Adverbial clauses of purpose indicate the intention someone has when doing something and is introduced by conjunctions such as 'to', 'in order to', 'so as to', 'so', 'so that', as in 'He did that just to upset her', 'They will have to work long hours in order to make that amount of money', 'They started to run so as to get home before it rained' and 'The firm reduced the number of staff in order that they might avoid bankruptcy'.

Adverbial clauses of reason explain why something happens or is done and are introduced by conjunctions such as 'because', 'since', 'as', as in 'We didn't go because the car broke down', 'As it was raining we had the party indoors' and 'since he has broken the school rules he should be punished'.

Adverbial clauses of result indicate the result of an event or situation and are introduced by the conjunctions 'so' or 'so that', as in 'He fell awkwardly so that he broke his leg' and 'She stumbled over her words so that the audience had difficulty understanding her'. *See* COMPARISON OF ADVERBS and COMPOUNDS.

aero- is a prefix meaning 'air', as in 'aerobics', 'aerodynamics', 'aeroplane' and 'aerospace', or 'aircraft', as in as in 'aerodrome', 'aeronaut',

affix refers to an element that is added to a base or root word to form another word. **Affixes** can be in the form of 'prefixes' or 'suffixes'. 'Prefix' is an **affix** that is added to the beginning of a word. Thus *audio* in 'audiovisual' is both a prefix and an affix. 'Suffix' is an **affix** that is added to the end of a word. Thus *-aholic* in 'workaholic' is a 'suffix' and an **affix.**

agent noun refers to someone that is the 'doer' of the action of a verb. It is usually spelt ending in either *-er*, as 'enquirer', or in *-or*, as in 'investigator' and 'supervisor', but frequently either of these endings is acceptable, as 'adviser/advisor'.

agreement or **concord** refers to the agreeing of two or more elements in a clause or sentence, i.e. they take the same number, person or gender. In English the most common form of **agreement** is that between subject and verb, and this usually involves **number agreement**. This means that singular nouns are usually accompanied by singular verbs, as in 'She looks well', 'He is working late' and 'The boy has passed the exam', and that plural nouns are usually accompanied by plural verbs, as in 'They look well', 'They are working late' and 'The boys have passed the exam'.

Problems arise when the noun in question can be either singular or plural, for example, 'audience', 'committee', 'crowd', 'family', 'government', 'group'. Such nouns take a singular verb if the user is regarding the people or items referred to by the noun as a group, as in 'The family is moving house', or as individuals, as in 'The family are quarrelling over where to go on holiday'.

Compound subjects, that is two or more nouns acting as the subject, whether singular or plural, joined with 'and', are used with a plural noun, as in 'My friend and I are going to the cinema tonight' and 'James and John are leaving today', unless the two nouns together represent a single concept, as 'brandy and soda', in which case the verb is in the singular, as in 'Brandy and soda is his favourite drink' and 'cheese and pickle' in 'Cheese and pickle is the only sandwich filing available.

In cases where two or more singular nouns acting as the subject are connected with such phrases as 'as well as', 'together with' and 'plus', as in 'His mother, as well as his father, is away from home' and 'The flat, together with the house, is up for sale', the verb is in the singular.

Indefinite pronouns such as 'anyone', 'everyone', 'no one', 'someone', 'either', 'neither' are singular and should be followed by a singular verb, as in 'Each of the flats is self-contained', 'Everyone is welcome', 'No one is allowed in without a ticket' and 'Neither is quite what I am looking for'.

When the subject is a singular noun, which is separated from the verb by a number of plural nouns, as in 'a list of dates and times of the next concerts', the verb is in the singular because 'list' is singular, as in 'A list of dates and times of the next concerts is available'.

Agreement with reference to both number and gender affects pronouns, as in 'She blames herself', 'He could have kicked himself' and 'They asked themselves why they had got involved'. Problems arise when the pronoun is indefinite and so the sex of the person is unspecified. Formerly in such cases the masculine pronouns were assumed to be neutral and so 'Each of the pupils was asked to hand in his work' was considered quite acceptable. The rise of feminism has led to a questioning of this assumption and alternatives have been put forward. These include 'Each of the pupils was asked to hand in his/her (or his or her) work', but some people feel that this is clumsy. Another alternative is 'Each of the pupils was asked to hand in their work'. Although it is ungrammatical, this convention is becoming quite acceptable in modern usage. To avoid both the clumsiness of the former and the ungrammaticalness of the latter, it is possible to cast the whole sentence in the plural, as in 'All the pupils were asked to hand in their work'.

agro-, agri- is a prefix derived from Greek meaning 'field', as in 'agriculture', 'agribusiness', 'agrobiology', 'agrochemicals'.

-aholic is a suffix meaning 'addicted to', formed on analogy with 'alcoholic', as in 'workaholic', 'shopaholic'. It sometimes becomes *-oholic*, as in *chocoholic*.

allegory is a kind of story which has deeper significance as well as the obvious surface meaning of the story. It is usually used to get a moral message across symbolically. Two of the famous allegories in English literature are *Pilgrim's Progress* by John Bunyan (1628-88) and *The Faerie Queene* by Edmund Spenser (1552-99).

alliteration is a figure of speech in which a sequence of words begin with the same letter or sound as in 'Round and round the rugged rocks the ragged rascal ran' and 'Peter Piper picked a peck of pickled peppers'. The given examples are both tongue twisters but **alliteration** is frequently used by poets for literary effect as in a 'red, red rose'.

also is an adverb and should not be used as a conjunction instead of 'and'. Thus sentences such as 'Please send me some apples, also some pears' are grammatically incorrect.

although is a conjunction used to introduce a 'subordinate adverbial clause of concession', as in 'They are very happy although they are poor', meaning 'Despite the fact they are poor they are happy'. 'Though' or 'even though' can be substituted for 'although', as in 'they are very happy even though they are poor'. *See* ADVERBIAL CLAUSE and CONJUNCTION.

ambi- is a prefix derived from Greek 'two', 'both', as in 'ambidextrous', 'ambivalent'.

an *see* **indefinite article**.

an- *see* **a-**.

-ana is a suffix meaning 'things associated with', as in 'Victoriana', 'Americana'.

anacoluthon is a figure of speech which refers to a change of construction in a sentence before the original structure is complete, as in 'My feeling is—but you must decide for yourself—how long did you say you have?' Anacoluthon is usually found in spoken English when someone is thinking aloud. Unlike many figures of speech, it is usually used accidentally rather than for literary or rhetorical effect.

anadiplosis is a figure of speech which refers to the repetition of a word or group at the end of one phrase or sentence and the beginning of the next for literary effect, as in 'sit and think about the past—the past which had been so warm and happy'.

analogy is a figure of speech rather like the simile in which there is an inference of a resemblance between two items that are being compared, as in 'Mary's parties are a bit like Christmas—much looked forward to but often a bit of a disappointment'.

anastrophe is a figure of speech which refers to an inversion of the usual order of words in a sentence or phrase for emphasis, or literary or rhetorical effect, as in 'Many a foreign dawn has he seen'.

and is called a coordinating conjunction because it joins elements of language which are of equal status. The elements may be words, as in 'cows and horses', 'John and

James', 'provide wine and beer'; phrases, as in 'working hard and playing hard' and 'trying to look after her children and her elderly parents'; clauses, as in 'John has decided to emigrate and his brother has decided to join him' and 'He has lost his job and he now has no money'. When a coordinating conjunction is used, the subject of the second clause can sometimes be omitted if it is the same as the subject of the first clause, as in 'They have been forced to sell the house and are very sad about it'. *See* CONJUNCTION.

The use of **and** at the beginning of a sentence is disliked by many people. It should be used only for deliberate effect, as in 'And then he saw the monster', or in informal contexts.

Other coordinating conjunctions include 'but', 'or', 'yet', 'both... and', 'either... or', and 'neither.... nor', as in 'poor but honest' and 'the blue dress or the green one'.

Anglo- is a prefix meaning 'English', as in 'Anglo-Irish', 'Anglo-Indian'.

ante- is a prefix derived from Latin meaning 'before', as in 'antedate', 'antenatal', 'anteroom'.

antecedent refers to the noun or noun phrase in a main clause to which a relative pronoun in a relative clause refers back. Thus in the sentence 'People who live dangerously frequently get hurt', 'people' is an antecedent. Similarly, in the sentence 'The child identified the old man who attacked her', 'the old man' is the antecedent'. *See* RELATIVE CLAUSE.

anthropo- is a prefix derived from Greek meaning 'human being', as in anthropoid, anthropology.

anti- is a prefix derived from Greek meaning 'against'. It is used in many words that have been established in the language for a long time, as in 'antidote' and 'antipathy', but it has also been used to form modern words, as 'anti-establishment', 'antifreeze', 'anti-inflationary', 'anti-nuclear', 'anti-warfare'.

anticlimax is a figure of speech in which there is a sudden descent from the lofty to the ridiculous or the trivial, as in 'She went home in a flood of tears and a taxi' and Alexander Pope's 'When husbands or when lapdogs breathe their last'.

antiphrasis is a figure of speech in which a word or phrase is used in a sense that is opposite to the accepted sense. It is often used to achieve an ironic or humorous effect, as in 'His mother is ninety years young today'. Young is usually associated with youth but here it is associated with old age.

antithesis is a figure of speech in contrasting ideas are balanced for effect, as in 'We need money, not advice', 'More haste, less speed' and 'Marry at haste, repent at leisure'. It is a common figure of speech in literature, as in Alexander Pope's 'To err is human, to forgive, divine' and John Milton's 'Better to reign in hell than to serve in heaven'.

antonomasia is a figure of speech indicating the use of a personal name or proper name to anyone belonging to a class or group, as in 'John is such an Einstein that the other members of the class are in awe of him', where the meaning is that 'John has such a brilliant mind that the other members of the class are in awe of him'.

antonym refers to a word that is the opposite of another word. Thus 'black' is an antonym for 'white', 'cowardly' is an antonym for 'courageous' , 'dull' is an antonym for 'bright', and 'fast' is an antonym for 'slow'.

any is a pronoun which may take either a singular or plural verb, depending on the context. When a singular noun is used, a singular verb is used, as in 'Is any of the cloth still usable?' 'Are any of the children coming?' When a plural noun is used, either a plural or a singular verb can be used, the singular verb being more formal, as in 'Did you ask if any of his friends were/was there?'.

anyone should be used with a singular verb, as in 'Has anyone seen my book' and 'Is anyone coming to the lecture'. It should also be followed, where relevant, by a singular, not plural, personal pronoun or possessive adjective, as in 'Has anyone left his/her book'. Because this construction, which avoids the sexist 'his', is considered by many people to be clumsy, there is a growing tendency to use 'their' and be ungrammatical.

aposiopesis is a figure of speech in which words are omitted or there is a sudden breaking off for dramatic effect, as in 'The door slowly opened and....' and 'There was the noise of gunshot and then....'

apostrophe[1] is a figure of speech which takes the form of a rhetorical address to an absent or dead person or to a personified thing, as in 'O Romeo! Romeo! wherefore art thou, Romeo?' and 'Oh Peace, why have you deserted us?'

apostrophe² is a form of punctuation that is mainly used to indicate possession. Many spelling errors centre on the position of the apostrophe in relation to *s*.

Possessive nouns are usually formed by adding *'s* to the singular noun, as in 'the girl's mother', and Peter's car'; by adding an apostrophe to plural nouns that end in *s*, as in 'all the teachers' cars'; by adding *'s* to irregular plural nouns that do not end in *s*, as in 'women's shoes'.

In the possessive form of a name or singular noun that ends in *s*, *x* or *z*, the apostrophe may or may not be followed by *s*. In words of one syllable the final *s* is usually added, as in 'James's house', 'the fox's lair', 'Roz's dress'. The final *s* is most frequently omitted in names, particularly in names of three or more syllables, as in 'Euripides' plays'. In many cases the presence or absence of final *s* is a matter of convention.

The apostrophe is also used to indicate omitted letters in contracted forms of words, as in 'can't' and 'you've'. They are sometimes used to indicate missing century numbers in dates, as in 'the '60s and '70s', but are not used at the end of decades, etc, as in '1960s', not '1960's'.

Generally apostrophes are no longer used to indicate omitted letters in shortened forms that are in common use, as in 'phone' and 'flu'.

Apostrophes are often omitted wrongly in modern usage, particularly in the media and by advertisers, as in 'womens hairdressers', 'childrens helpings'. In addition, apostrophes are frequently added erroneously (as in 'potato's for sale' and 'Beware of the dog's'). This is partly because people are unsure about when and when not to use them and partly because of a modern tendency to punctuate as little as possible.

apposition refers to a noun or a phrase which provides further information about another noun or phrase. Both nouns and phrases refer to the same person or thing. In the phrase 'Peter Jones, our managing director', ' Peter Jones' and 'our managing director' are said to be in **apposition**. Similarly, in the phrase 'his cousin, the chairman of the firm', 'his cousin' and 'the chairman of the firm' are in **apposition.**

arch- is a prefix derived from Greek meaning 'chief', as in 'archbishop', 'archduke', 'arch-enemy'.

-arch is a suffix derived from the Greek meaning 'chief, ruler', as in 'anarchy', 'hierarchy' and 'monarchy'.

-arian is a suffix derived from Latin and means, in one of its senses, 'a supporter of', as in 'vegetarian', or 'one connected with', as in 'antiquarian' and 'librarian'.

article *see* **definite article** and **indefinite article.**

as is a conjunction which can introduce either a 'subordinate adverbial clause of time', as in 'I caught sight of him as I was leaving', a 'subordinate adverbial clause of manner', as in 'He acted as he promised', and 'a subordinate adverbial clause of reason', as in 'As it's Saturday he doesn't have to work'. it is also used in the **as....as** construction, as in 'She doesn't play as well as her sister does'.

The construction may be followed by a subject pro-

noun or an object pronoun, according to sense. In the
sentence 'He plays as well as she', which is a slightly
shortened form of 'She plays as well as he does', 'he' is
a subject pronoun. In informal English the subject pronoun often becomes an object pronoun, as in 'She plays
as well as him'. In the sentence 'They hate their father
as much as her', 'her' is an object and the sentence means
'They hate their father as much as they hate her', but in
the sentence 'They hate their father as much as she', 'she'
is a subject and the sentence means 'They hate their father as much as she does'. *See* ADVERBIAL CLAUSE and
CONJUNCTION.

assonance is a figure of speech in which vowel sounds
are repeated to give a half-rhyme effect, as in 'with gun,
drum, trumpet, blunderbuss and thunder'.

astro- is a prefix derived from Greek meaning 'star', as in
'astrology', 'astronomy', 'astronaut', 'astrophysics'.

asyndeton is a figure of speech referring to the omission
of conjunctions for dramatic or literary effect, as in 'I
came, I saw, I conquered' and 'He entered, he looked
round, he left'.

-athon, -thon is a suffix meaning 'large scale or long-
lasting contest or event', as in 'swimathon', 'telethon'.
These words are formed on analogy with the Greek derived word 'marathon', and they often refer to events
undertaken for charity.

attributive adjective refers to an **adjective** that is placed
immediately before the noun which it qualifies. In the
phrases 'a red dress', 'the big house' and 'an enjoyable

31

evening', 'red, 'big' and 'enjoyable' are attributive adjectives.

audio- is derived from Latin 'hear'. It is found in several words that have been established in the language for a long time, as in 'auditory', 'audition', but it is also used to form many modern words, as in 'audiotape', 'audiocassette' and 'audiovisual'.

auto- is a prefix derived from Greek meaning 'of or by itself', as in 'autobiography' and 'autograph'. It is also used to refer to things that work by themselves 'automatically', as in 'automobile', 'autocue', 'automaton', and to things that have to do with cars, as in 'automobiles', 'autosport', 'autotheft'.

auxiliary verb refers to a verb which is used in forming tenses, moods and voices of other verbs. These include 'be', 'do' and 'have'.

The verb 'to be' is used as an **auxiliary verb** with the -*ing* form of the main verb to form the continuous present tense, as in 'They are living abroad just now' and 'We were thinking of going on holiday but we changed our minds'.

The verb 'to be' is used as an **auxiliary verb** with the past participle of the main verb to form the passive voice, as in 'Her hands were covered in blood' and 'These toys are manufactured in China'.

The verb 'to have' is used as an **auxiliary verb** along with the past participle of the main verb to form the perfect tenses, as in 'They have filled the post', 'She had realized her mistake' and 'They wished that they had gone earlier'.

The verb 'to be' is used as an **auxiliary verb** along with the main verb to form negative sentences, as in 'She is not accepting the job'. The verb 'to do' is used as an **auxiliary verb** along with the main verb to form negative sentences, as in 'he does not believe her'. It is also used along with the main verb to form questions, as in 'Does he know that she's gone?' and to form sentences in which the verb is emphasized, as in 'She *does* want to go'. *See* **modal auxiliary**.

B

back formation refers to the process of forming a new word by removing an element from an existing word. This is the reversal of the usual process since many words are formed by adding an element to a base or root word. Examples of **back formation** include 'burgle' from 'burglary'; 'caretake' from 'caretaker'; 'donate' from 'donation; 'eavesdrop' from 'eavesdropper'; 'enthuse' from 'enthusiasm'; 'intuit' from 'intuition'; 'liaise' from 'liaison'; 'reminisce' from 'reminiscence'; 'televise' from 'television'.

base refers to the basic uninflected form of a verb. It is found as the infinitive form, as in 'to go' and 'to take', and as the imperative form, as in 'Go away!' and 'Take it!' It is also the form that the verb in the present indicative tense takes, except for the third person singular, as in 'I always go there on a Sunday' and 'They go there regularly.' **Base** also refers to the basic element in word formation. In this sense it is also known as 'root' or 'stem'. For example, in 'infectious' 'infect' is the base, in 'indescribable' 'describe' is the base and in 'enthusiastic' 'enthuse' is the base.

bathos is a figure of speech consisting of sudden descent from the lofty or noble to the ridiculous or trivial. This descent can be either intentional for comic or satiric effect, as in Alexander Pope's 'When husbands or when lapdogs breathe their last', or it can be accidental, as in 'She collected her children and her coat'. **Bathos** and 'anticlimax' mean the same. *See* **anticlimax**.

be *see* **auxiliary verb**.

both can be used as determiner, as in 'He broke both his arms' and 'He lost both his sons in the war'; a pronoun, as in 'I don't mind which house we rent. I like them both' and 'Neither of them work here. The boss sacked them both'; a conjunction, as in 'He both likes and admires her' and 'She is both talented and honest'. **Both** can sometimes be followed by 'of'. 'Both their children are grown up' and 'Both of their children are grown up' are both acceptable. Care should be taken to avoid using **both** unnecessarily. In the sentence 'The two items are both identical', **both** is redundant.

because is a conjunction that introduces a subordinate adverbial clause of reason', as in 'They sold the house because they are going abroad' and 'Because she is shy she never goes to parties'. It is often used incorrectly in such constructions as 'The reason they went away is because they were bored'. This should be rephrased as either 'The reason that they went away is that they were bored' or 'They went away because they were bored'.

before can either be a preposition, an adverb or a conjunction. As a preposition it means either 'coming or going in front of in time', as in 'He was the chairman before this one', or coming or going in front of in place, as in 'She went before him into the restaurant'. As an adverb it means 'at a time previously', as in 'I told you before' and 'He has been married before'. As a conjunction it introduces a 'subordinate adverbial clause of time', as in 'The guests arrived before she was ready for them' and 'Before I knew it they had arrived'.

bi- is a prefix derived from Latin meaning 'two', as in 'bicycle', 'bifocal', 'bilingual', 'binoculars', 'bisect'. Bi- forms words in English in which it means 'half', and other words in which it means 'twice'. This can give rise to confusion in such words as 'biweekly' and 'bimonthly', where there are two possible sets of meanings. 'Biweekly' can mean either 'every two weeks' or 'twice a week' so that one would not be able to be certain about the frequency of a 'biweekly' publication. Similarly, a 'bimonthly' publication might appear either twice a month or once every two months.

biblio- is a prefix derived from Greek meaning 'book', as in 'bibliophile' (a person who is fond of or collects books) and 'bibliography'.

bio- is a prefix derived from Greek meaning life or living material, as in 'biography', 'biology', 'biochemistry', 'biodegradable', 'biosphere', 'biopsy'.

blend refers to a word formed by the merging of two other words or elements, as in 'brunch' from 'breakfast' and 'lunch'; 'camcorder' from 'camera' and 'recorder'; 'chocoholic' from 'chocolate' and 'alcoholic'; 'motel' from 'motor' and 'hotel'; 'smog' from 'smoke' and 'fog';

'televangelist' from 'television' and 'evangelist'.

bold or **bold face** refers to a typeface that is thick and black. It is used for emphasis or to highlight certain words. The headwords or entry words in this book are set in bold type.

book titles cause problems as to punctuation. How they are treated in publications, business reports, etc, depends largely on the house style of the firm concerned. However, they are generally written in documents, letters, etc, as they appear on their title pages, that is with the first letter of the first word and of the following main words of the title in capital letters, and those of words of lesser importance, such as the articles, prepositions and coordinate conjunctions, in lowercase letters, as in The Guide to Yoga, Hope for the Best and In the Middle of Life.

Some people, and some house-style manuals, prefer to put the titles in italic, as in *A Room with a View* and *A Guide to Dental Health*. Others prefer to put book titles in quotation marks, as in 'Gardening for Beginners'. Such a convention can make use of either single or double quotation marks. Thus either 'Desserts for the Summer' or "Desserts for the Summer" is possible provided that the writer is consistent throughout any one piece of writing. If the title of a book is mentioned in a piece of direct speech in quotation marks it goes within the opposite style of quotation marks from the piece in direct speech. Thus if the direct speech is within single quotation marks, the book title goes within double quotation marks, as in

'Have you read "Wuthering Heights" or are you not a Bronte fan?' If the direct speech is within double quotation marks, the book title goes between single quotation marks, as in "Would you say that 'Animal Farm' was your favourite Orwell novel?"

It is even quite common for book titles to appear in documents both in italic type and with quotation marks. To some extent the punctuation of book titles is a matter of choice as long as they are consistent, but there is a growing tendency to have as little punctuation as possible and to have as uncluttered a page as possible.

borrowing refers to the taking over of a word from a foreign language and also refers to the word so borrowed. Many words borrowed into English are totally assimilated as to spelling and pronunciation. Others remain obviously different and retain their own identity as to spelling or pronunciation, as 'raison d'être', borrowed from French. Many of them have been so long part of the English language, such as since the Norman Conquest, that they are no longer thought of as being foreign words. However the process goes on, and recent borrowings include 'glasnost' and 'perestroika' from Russian.

French, Latin and Greek have been the main sources of our **borrowings** over the centuries. However, we have borrowed extensively from other languages as well. These include Italian, from which we have borrowed many terms relating to music, art and architecture. These include 'piano', 'libretto', 'opera', 'soprano', 'tempo', 'corridor', 'fresco', 'niche', 'parapet' and 'grotto', as well as many food terms such as 'macaroni', 'pasta', 'semolina' and 'spaghetti'.

From the Dutch we have acquired many words relating to the sea and ships since they were a great sea-faring nation. These include 'cruise', 'deck', 'skipper' and 'yacht'. Through the Dutch/Afrikaans connection we have borrowed 'apartheid', 'boss' and 'trek'.

From German we have borrowed 'dachshund', 'hamster', 'frankfurter', 'kindergarten' and 'waltz', as well as some words relating to World War II, for example, 'blitz', 'flak' and 'strafe'.

From Norse and the Scandinavian languages have come a wide variety of common words, such as 'egg', 'dirt', 'glitter', 'kick', 'law', 'odd', 'skill', 'take', 'they', 'though', as well as some more modern sporting terms such as 'ski' and 'slalom'.

From the Celtic languages have come 'bannock', 'bog', 'brogue', 'cairn', 'clan', 'crag', 'slogan' and 'whisky', and from Arabic have come 'algebra', 'alkali', 'almanac', 'apricot', 'assassin', 'cypher', 'ghoul', 'hazard', 'mohair', 'safari', 'scarlet' and 'talisman'.

The Indian languages have provided us with many words, originally from the significant British presence there in the days of the British Empire. They include 'bungalow', 'chutney', 'dinghy', 'dungarees', 'gymkhana', 'jungle', 'pundit' and 'shampoo'. In modern times there has been an increasing interest in Indian food and cookery, and words such as 'pakora', 'poppadom', 'samosa', etc, have come into the language.

From the South American languages have come 'avocado', 'chocolate', 'chilli', 'potato', 'tobacco' and 'tomato'. From Hebrew have come 'alphabet', 'camel', 'cinnamon' and 'maudlin', as well as more modern borrowings from Yiddish such as 'bagel', 'chutzpah', 'schmaltz' and 'schmuck'.

From the native North American languages have come 'anorak', 'kayak', 'raccoon' and 'toboggan', and from the Aboriginal language of Australia have come 'boomerang' and 'kangaroo'.

'Judo', 'bonsai', and 'tycoon' have come from Japanese, 'rattan' from Malay and 'kung-fu', 'sampan' and 'ginseng' from Chinese.

The borrowing process continues. With Britain becoming more of a cosmopolitan and multi-cultural nation the borrowing is increasing.

-bound is a suffix meaning 'confined or restricted', as in housebound, snowbound and spellbound. It can also mean 'obligated', as in 'duty-bound'.

brackets are used to enclose information that is in some way additional to the main statement. The information so enclosed is called 'parenthesis' and the pair of brackets enclosing it can be known as 'parentheses'. The information that is enclosed in the brackets is purely supplementary or explanatory in nature and could be removed without changing the overall basic meaning or grammatical completeness of the statement. **Brackets**, like 'commas' and 'dashes', interrupt the flow of the main statement but **brackets** indicate a more definite or clear-cut interruption. The fact that they are more visually obvious emphasizes this.

Material within brackets can be one word, as in 'In a local wine bar we had some delicious crepes (pancakes)' and 'They didn't have the chutzpah (nerve) to challenge her'. It can also take the form of dates, as in 'Robert Louis Stevenson (1850-94) wrote *Treasure Island*' and '*Animal Farm* was written by George Orwell (1903-50)'.

The material within brackets can also take the form of a phrase, as in 'They served lasagne (a kind of pasta) and some delicious veal' and 'They were drinking Calvados (a kind of brandy made from apples)' or in the form of a clause, as in 'We were to have supper (or so they called it) later in the evening' and 'They went for a walk round the loch (as a lake is called in Scotland) before taking their departure'.

It can also take the form of a complete sentence, as in 'He was determined (we don't know why) to tackle the problem alone' and 'She made it clear (nothing could be more clear) that she was not interested in the offer'. Sentences that appear in brackets in the middle of a sentence are not usually given an initial capital letter or a full stop, as in 'They very much desired (she had no idea why) to purchase her house'. If the material within brackets comes at the end of a sentence the full stop comes outside the second bracket, as in 'For some reason we agreed to visit her at home (we had no idea where she lived)'.

buildings

If the material in the brackets is a sentence which comes between two other sentences it is treated like a normal sentence with an initial capital letter and a closing full stop, as in 'He never seems to do any studying. (He is always either asleep or watching television.) Yet he does brilliantly in his exams.' Punctuation of the main statement is unaffected by the presence of the brackets and their enclosed material except that any punctuation that would have followed the word before the first bracket follows the second bracket, as in 'He lives in a place (I am not sure exactly where), that is miles from anywhere.

There are various shapes of brackets. Round brackets are the most common type. Square brackets are sometimes used to enclose information that is contained inside other information already in brackets, as in '(Christopher Marlowe [1564-93] was a contemporary of Shakespeare)' or in a piece of writing where round brackets have already been used for some other purpose. Thus in a dictionary if round brackets are used to separate off the pronunciation, square brackets are sometimes used to separate off the etymologies.

Square brackets are also used for editorial comments in a scholarly work where the material within brackets is more of an intrusion to the flow of the main statement than is normerly the case with bracketed material. Angle brackets and brace brackets tend to be used in more scholarly or technical contexts.

buildings can cause problems with regard to the style and punctuation of their names. The proper name attached

to the building should have an initial capital, as should
the common noun that may be part of it, as in The White
House, The Saltire Building, The National Portrait Gal-
lery and The Museum of Childhood.

businesses and **organizations** often cause style and punctuation problems with regard to their names or titles. In
general the initial letters of the main words of the title
should be in capital letters and the words of lesser importance, such as the articles, coordinating conjunctions
and prepositions, should be in lower case, except when
they are the first word of the title, as in 'The Indian Carpet Company', 'Kitchens for All' and 'Capital Indus-
trial Cleaners'. Obviously, when the names of people
are involved these should have initial capital letters, as
in 'Jones and Brown'.

but is a conjunction that connects two opposing ideas. It
is a 'coordinating conjunction' in that it connects two
elements of equal status. The elements may be words, as
in 'not James but John'; phrases, as in 'working hard
but not getting anywhere' and 'trying to earn a living
but not succeeding'; clauses, as in 'He has arrived but
his sister is late', 'I know her but I have never met him'
and 'He likes reading but she prefers to watch TV'. It
should not be used when no element of contrast is present.
Thus the following sentence should be rephrased, at least
in formal English—'She is not professionally trained but
taught herself'. The two clauses are in fact agreeing, not
disagreeing, with each other and so, strictly speaking,
but should not be used.

by-

The use of **but** at the beginning of a sentence is disliked by many people. It should be used only for deliberate effect or in informal contexts.

by- is a prefix meaning 'subordinate', 'secondary', 'incidental', as in by-product, by-road, by-effect. It can also mean 'around', as in by-pass.

C

capital letters are much less common than lower-case letters. They are used as the initial letter of proper nouns. Thus names of countries, rivers, mountains, cities, etc. Thus we find Africa, Mount Everest, River Nile, Paris, etc. The first names and surnames of people have initial capital letters, as in John Black and Mary Brown. Initial capital letters are used for the days of the week, as in Tuesday and Wednesday, for the months of the year, as in May and October, public and religious holidays, as in Easter Sunday, Ramadan and Hanaku. Initial capital letters are used for the books of the Bible.

Points of the compass are spelt with an initial capital letter if they are part of a specific geographical feature or region, as in South Africa.

Initial capital letters are usually used in the titles of books. Only the main words are capitalized. Prepositions, determiners and the articles are left in lower-case, unless they form the first word of the title, as in *A Room with a View* and *For Whom the Bell Tolls—see* BOOK TITLES.

Initial capital letters are necessary in tradenames, as in Hoover, Jacuzzi, Xerox and Kodak. Note that verbs formed from trade names are not spelt with an initial capital letter.

The first word in a sentence is spelt with a capital letter, as in 'We heard them come in. They made very little noise. However, we are light sleepers.'.

For capital letters in direct speech see DIRECT SPEECH. For capital letters in abbreviation and acronyms see ABBREVIATIONS and ACRONYMS.

cardi- is a prefix derived from Greek meaning 'heart', as in 'cardiology', 'cardiac'.

cardinal number refers to numbers such as one, two three, etc, as opposed to 'ordinal numbers' which refer to numbers such as first, second, third, etc.

clause refers to a group of words containing a finite verb which forms part of a compound or complex sentence. See MAIN CLAUSE, SUBORDINATE CLAUSES, ADVERBIAL CLAUSES, NOUN CLAUSES and RELATIVE clauses.

clerihew is a humorous four-line light verse in which the first two lines rhyme with each other and the last two rhyme with each other. The clerihew was popularized by Edward Clerihew Bentley (1875-1956). It usually deals with a person named in the first line and then describes him in a humorous way, as in

> Mr Michael Foot
> Had lots of loot
> He loved to gloat
> While petting his stoat

cliché is a hackneyed stereotyped expression which is much overused. Examples of clichés include 'unaccustomed as I am to public speaking', 'the light at the end of the tunnel' and 'All's well that ends well'.

collective noun refers to a group of things or people. It is used when the whole group is being considered, as in 'flock of sheep', 'herd of cattle', 'team of oxen', 'shoal of herring', 'covey of partridges', 'unkindness of ravens', 'gaggle of geese', 'pride of lions', 'mutation of thrushes', 'exaltation of larks', 'convocation of eagles'.

colloquial refers to informal language, such as that found in informal conversation.

colon is a punctuation mark (:) which is used within a sentence to explain, interpret, clarify or amplify what has gone before it. 'The standard of school work here is extremely high: it is almost university standard', 'The fuel bills are giving cause for concern: they are almost double last year's'. 'We have some new information: the allies have landed'. A capital letter is not usually used after the colon in this context.

The **colon** is also used to introduce lists or long quotations, as in 'The recipe says we need: tomatoes, peppers, courgettes, garlic, oregano and basil', 'The boy has a huge list of things he needs for school: blazer, trousers, shirts, sweater, ties, shoes, tennis shoes, rugby boots, sports clothes and leisure wear' and 'One of his favourite quotations was: "If music be the food of love play on"'.

The **colon** is sometimes used in numerals, as in '7:30 a.m.', '22:11:72' and 'a ratio of 7:3'. It is used in the titles of some books, for example where there is a subtitle or explanatory title, as in 'The Dark Years: the Economy in the 1930s.

In informal writing, the dash is sometimes used instead of the colon. Indeed the dash tends to be overused for this purpose.

comma is a very common punctuation mark. In modern usage there is a tendency to adopt a system of minimal punctuation and the comma is one of the casualties of this new attitude. Most people use the comma considerably less frequently than was formerly the case.

However there are certain situations in which the comma is still commonly used. One of these concerns lists. The individual items in a series of three or more items are separated by commas. Whether a comma is put before the 'and' which follows the second-last item is now a matter of choice. Some people dislike the use of a comma after 'and' in this situation, and it was formerly considered wrong. Examples of lists include—'at the sports club we can play tennis, squash, badminton and table tennis', 'We need to buy bread, milk, fruit and sugar', and 'They are studying French, German, Spanish and Russian'. The individual items in a list can be quite long, as in 'We opened the door, let ourselves in, fed the cat and started to cook a meal' and 'They consulted the map, planned the trip, got some foreign currency and were gone before we realized it'. Confusion may arise if the last item in the list contains 'and' in its own right, as in 'In the pub they served ham salad, shepherd's pie, pie and chips and omelette. In such cases it as well to put a comma before the 'and'.

In cases where there is a list of adjectives before a noun,

the use of commas is now optional although it was formerly standard practice. Thus both 'She wore a long, red, sequinned dress' and 'She wore a long red sequinned dress' are used. When the adjective immediately before the noun has a closer relationship with it than the other adjectives no comma should be used, as in 'a beautiful old Spanish village'.

The **comma** is used to separate clauses or phrases that are parenthetical or naturally cut off from the rest of a sentence, as in 'My mother, who was of Irish extraction, was very superstitious'. In such a sentence the clause within the commas can be removed without altering the basic meaning. Care should be taken to include both commas. Commas are not normally used to separate main clauses and relative clauses, as in 'The woman whom I met was my friend's sister'. Nor are they usually used to separate main clauses and subordinate clauses, as in 'He left when we arrived' and 'They came to the party although we didn't expect them to'. If the subordinate clause precedes the main clause, it is sometimes followed by a comma, especially if it is a reasonably long clause, as in 'Although we stopped and thought about it, we still made the wrong decision'. If the clause is quite short, or if it is a short phrase, a comma is not usually inserted, as in 'Although it rained we had a good holiday' and 'Although poor they were happy'. The use of commas to separate such words and expression from the rest of the sentence to which they are related is optional. Thus one can write 'However, he could be right' or 'However he could be right'. The longer the expression is, the more likely it is to have a comma after it, as in 'On the other hand, we may decide not to go'.

Commas are always used to separate terms of address, interjections or question tags from the rest of the sentence, as in 'Please come this way, Ms Brown, and make yourself at home', 'Now, ladies, what can I get you?' and 'It's cold today, isn't it?'

Commas may be used to separate main clauses joined by a coordinating conjunction, but this is not usual if the clauses have the same subject or object, as in 'She swept the floor and dusted the table'. In cases where the subjects are different and the clauses are fairly long, it is best to insert a comma, as in 'They took all the furniture with them, and she was left with nothing'.

A **comma** can be inserted to avoid repeating a verb in the second of two clause, as in 'he plays golf and tennis, his brother rugby'.

commands are expressed in the imperative mood, as in 'Be quiet!', 'Stop crying!', 'Go away!'

common nouns are simply the names of ordinary, everyday non-specific things and people, as opposed to proper nouns which refer to the names of particular individuals or specific places. **Common nouns** include 'baby', 'cat', 'girl', 'hat', 'park', 'sofa' and 'table'.

comparison of adjectives is achieved in two different ways. Some adjectives form their comparative by adding -er to the positive or absolute form, as in 'braver', 'louder', 'madder', 'shorter' and 'taller'. Other adjectives form their comparative by using 'more' in conjunction with them, as in 'more beautiful', 'more realistic', 'more suitable', and 'more tactful'. Which is the correct form is largely a matter of length. One-syllable adjectives, such as 'loud', add *-er*, as 'louder'. Two-syllable adjectives sometimes have both forms as a possibility, as in 'gentler/more gentle', and 'cleverest/most clever'. Adjectives with three or more syllables usually form their comparatives with 'more', as in 'more comfortable', 'more gracious', 'more regular', and 'more understanding'. Some adjectives are irregular in their comparative forms, as in 'good/better', 'bad/worse', 'many/more'. Only if they begin with *un-* are they likely to end in *-er*, as in 'untrustworthier'.

Some adjectives by their very definitions do not normally have a comparative form, for example 'unique'.

complement is the equivalent of 'object' in a clause with a linking or copula verb. In the sentence 'Jack is a policeman', 'a policeman' is the **complement**. In the sentence 'Jane is a good mother', 'a good mother' is the complement', and in the sentence 'His son is an excellent football player', 'an excellent football player' is the complement.

complex sentence refers to a type of sentence in which there is a main clause and one or more subordinate clauses. The sentence 'We went to visit him although he had been unfriendly to us' is a complex sentence since it is composed of a main clause and one subordinate clause ('although he had been unfriendly to us'). The sentence

'We wondered where he had gone and why he was upset' is a complex sentence since it has a main clause and two subordinate clauses ('where he had gone' and 'why he was upset').

compound sentence refers to a type of sentence with more than one clause and linked by a coordinating conjunction, such as 'and' or 'but', as in 'He applied for a new job and got it' and 'I went to the cinema but I didn't enjoy the film'.

concord *see* **number agreement**.

concrete noun refers to something which one can touch, as opposed to an 'abstract noun' which one cannot. **Concrete nouns** include 'bag', 'glass', 'plate', 'pot', 'clothes', 'field', 'garden', 'flower', 'potato', 'foot' and 'shoe'. *See* ABSTRACT NOUN.

conjunctions are of two types. Coordinating conjunctions join units of equal status, as in 'bread and butter', 'We asked for some food and we got it'. A subordinating conjunction joins a dependent or subordinating clause to main verbs: in 'We asked him why he was there', 'why he was there' is a subordinate clause and thus 'why' is a subordinating conjunction.

continuous tenses *see* **tense**.

copula *see* **linking verb**.

copular verb *see* **linking verb**.

count noun is the same as COUNTABLE NOUN.

countable noun is one which can be preceded by 'a' and can take a plural, as in 'hat/hats', 'flower/flowers'. *See also* UNCOUNTABLE NOUN.

D

dangling participle is one that has been misplaced in a sentence. A participle is often used to introduce a phrase which is attached to a subject mentioned later in a sentence, as in 'Worn out by the long walk, she fell to the ground in a faint'. 'Worn out' is the participle and 'she' the subject. Another example is 'Laughing in glee at having won, she ordered some champagne'. In this sentence 'laughing' is the participle and 'she' is the subject. It is a common error for such a participle not to be related to any subject, as in 'Imprisoned in the dark basement, it seemed a long time since she had seen the sun'. This participle is said to be 'dangling'. Another example of a **dangling participle** is contained in 'Living alone, the days seemed long'.

It is also a common error for a participle to be related to the wrong subject in a sentence, as in 'Painting the ceiling, some of the plaster fell on his head', 'Painting' is the participle and should go with a subject 'he'. Instead it goes with 'some of the plaster'. Participles in this situation are more correctly known as 'misrelated participles', although they are also called **dangling participles.**

dash is a punctuation mark in the form of a short line that indicates a short break in the continuity of a sentence, as in 'He has never been any trouble at school—quite the reverse', 'I was amazed when he turned up—I thought he was still abroad'. In such situations it serves the same purpose as brackets, except that it is frequently considered more informal. The dash should be used sparingly. Depending on it too much can lead to careless writing with ideas set down at random rather than turned into a piece of coherent prose.

The **dash** can be used to emphasize a word or phrase, as in 'They said goodbye then—forever'. It can also be used to add a remark to the end of a sentence, as in 'They had absolutely no money—a regular state of affairs towards the end of the month.' The **dash** can also be used to introduce a statement that amplifies or explains what has been said, as in 'The burglars took everything of value—her jewellery, the silver, the TV set, her hi-fi and several hundred pounds.' It can be used to summarize what has gone before, as in 'Disease, poverty, ignorance—these are the problems facing us.'

The **dash** is also used to introduce an afterthought, as in 'You can come with me—but you might not want to'. It can also introduce a sharp change of subject, as in 'I'm just making tea—what was that noise?' It can also be used to introduce some kind of balance in a sentence, as in 'It's going to take two of us to get this table out of here—one to move it and one to hold the door open.'

The **dash** is sometimes found in pairs. A pair of dashes

acts in much the same way as a set of round brackets. A pair of dashes can be used to indicate a break in a sentence, as in 'We prayed—prayed as we had never prayed before—that the children would be safe', 'It was—on reflection—his best performance yet', and 'He introduced me to his wife—an attractive pleasant woman—before he left'.

Dashes are used to indicate hesitant speech, as in 'I don't—well—maybe—you could be right'. They can be used to indicate the omission of part of a word or name, as in 'It's none of your b—business.', 'He's having an affair with Mrs D–'.

They can also be used between points in time or space, as in 'Edinburgh—London' and '1750—1790.'

dates are usually written in figures, as in 1956, rather than in words, as in nineteen fifty-six, except in formal contexts, such as legal documents. There are various ways of writing dates. The standard form in Britain is becoming day followed by month followed by year, as in '24 February 1970'. In America the standard form of this is 'February 24 1970', and that is a possibility in Britain also. Alternatively, some people write '24th February 1970'. Care should be taken with the writing of dates entirely in numbers, especially if one is corresponding with someone in America. In Britain the day of the month is put first, the month second and the year third, as in '2/3/50', '2 March 1950'. In America the month is put first, followed by the day of the month and the year. Thus in America '2/3/50' would be 3 February 1950.

Centuries may be written either in figures, as in 'the 19th century', or in words, as in 'the nineteenth century'.

Decades and centuries are now usually written without apostrophes. as in '1980s' and '1990s'.

dative case refers to the case which indicates 'to' or 'for'. This is applicable to Latin but not to English, where such meanings are expressed by prepositional phrases. In English the 'indirect object' is equivalent to the **dative case** in some situations.

deca- is a prefix derived from Greek meaning 'ten', as in 'decade', 'decathlon' and 'decahedron'.

deci- is a prefix derived from Latin meaning 'tenth', as in 'decibel', 'decimal', 'decimate' and 'decilitre'.

declarative sentence refers to a sentence which conveys information. The subject precedes the verb in it. Examples include 'They won the battle', 'He has moved to another town', 'Lots of people go there' and 'There is a new person in charge'. **Declarative mood** is the same as **indicative mood**.

declension refers to the variation of the form of a noun, adjective or pronoun to show different cases, such as nominative and accusative. It also refers to the class into which such words are placed, as in first declension, second declension, etc. The term applies to languages such as Latin but is not applicable to English.

definite article is a term for 'the', which is the most frequently used word in the English language. 'The' is used to refer back to a person or thing that has already been mentioned, as in 'Jack and Jill built a model. The model was of a ship' and 'We've bought a car. It was the cheapest car we could find'.

'The' can be used to make a general statement about all things of a particular type, as in 'The computer has lead to the loss of many jobs' and 'The car has caused damage to the environment'. 'The' can be used to refer to a whole class or group, as in 'the Italians', 'the Browns' and 'the younger generation'.

'The' can also be used to refer to services or systems, as in 'They are not on the phone' and 'She prefers going by bus'. It can be used to refer to the name of a musical instrument when someone's ability to play it is being referred to, as in 'Her son is learning to play the violin'.

'The' indicates a person or thing to be the only one, as in the Bible, the King of Spain, the White House, the Palace of Westminster and the President of the United States.

'The' can be used instead of a possessive determiner to refer to parts of the body, as in 'She took him by the arm' and 'The dog bit him on the leg'.

'The' is used in front of superlative adjectives, as in 'the largest amount of money' and 'the most beautiful woman'. It can also be used to indicate that a person or thing is unique or exceptional, as in 'the political debater of his generation'. In this last sense 'the' is pronounced 'thee'.

degree refers to a level of comparison of gradable adjectives. The degrees of comparison comprise 'absolute' or 'positive', as in 'big', 'calm', 'dark', 'fair', 'hot', 'late', 'short' and 'tall'; 'comparative', as in 'bigger', 'calmer', 'darker', 'fairest', 'hotter', 'late', 'shorter' and 'taller'; 'superlative', as in 'biggest', 'calmest', 'darkest', 'fairest', 'hottest', 'latest', 'shortest' and 'tallest'.

Degree can also refer to adverbs. 'Adverbs of degree' include 'extremely', 'very', 'greatly', 'rather', 'really', 'remarkably', 'terribly', as in 'an extremely rare case', 'a very old man', 'He's remarkably brave' and 'We're terribly pleased'.

demi- is a prefix derived from old French meaning 'half', as in 'demigod' and 'demijohn'.

demonstrative determiners are used to indicate things or people in relationship to the speaker or writer in space or time. 'This' and 'these' indicate nearness to the speaker, as in 'Will you take this book home?' and 'These flowers are for you'. 'That' and 'those' indicate distance from the speaker, as in 'Get that creature out of here!' and 'Aren't those flowers over there beautiful!'

demonstrative pronouns are similar to **demonstrative determiners** except that they stand alone in place of a noun rather than preceding a noun, as in 'I'd like to give you this', 'What is that?', 'These are interesting books' and 'Those are not his shoes'.

dependent clause refers to a clause which cannot stand alone and make sense, unlike an independent or main clause. **Dependent clauses** depend on the main clause. The term is the same as 'subordinate clause'. *See* SUBORDINATE CLAUSE.

derivation has two meanings. It can refer to the etymology of a word, as in 'The derivation of the expression is unknown'. It can also refer to the process of forming a new word by adding an affix of some kind to an existing word or base, as in 'helpless' from 'help' and 'maker' from 'make'.

derivative refers to a word formed by **derivation**. For example, 'sweetly' is a derivative of 'sweet', 'peaceful' is a derivative from 'peace', 'clinging' from 'cling' and 'shortest' from 'short'.

derm- is a prefix derived from Greek meaning 'skin', as in 'dermatitis', 'dermatologist' and 'dermatology'.

determiner is a word used in front of a noun or pronoun to tell us something about it. Unlike an adjective, it does not, strictly speaking, 'describe' a noun or pronoun. **Determiners** are divided into the following categories— articles (a, an, the) as in 'a cat', 'an eagle', 'the book'; demonstrative determiners (this, that, these, those), as in 'this girl', 'that boy' and 'those people'; possessive determiners (my, your, his/her/its, our, their), as in 'my dog', 'her house', 'its colour', 'their responsibility'; numbers (one ,two, three, four, etc, first, second, third, fourth, etc), as in 'two reasons', 'five ways', 'ten children'; and indefinite or general determiners (all, another, any, both, each, either, enough, every, few, fewer, less, little, many, most, much, neither, no, other, several, some), as in 'both parents', 'enough food', 'several issues'. Many words used as determiners are also pronouns. *See* ADJECTIVE; DEMONSTRATIVE DETERMINER; POSSESSIVE DETERMINER; NUM-

di-

BERS; INDEFINITE DETERMINER.

di- is a prefix derived from Greek meaning 'two' or 'double', as in 'dioxide', 'dilemma', 'diphthong' and 'disyllabic'.

dia- is a prefix meaning 'through', as in 'diaphanous'; 'apart', as in 'diacritical', 'diaphragm' and 'dialysis'; and 'across', as in 'diameter'.

diacritic refers to a mark placed over, under or through a letter to indicate a sound or stress value different from that of the same letter when it is unmarked. **Diacritics** include the cedilla, as in 'façade', the German umlaut, as in 'mädchen' and diaeresis, as in 'naïve'.

diaeresis refers to a mark that is placed over a vowel to indicate that it is sounded separately from a neighbouring vowel, as in 'naïve', 'Chloë'.

dialect refers to a variety of language that is distinct from other varieties in terms of pronunciation, accent, vocabulary, grammar and sentence structure. The term **dialect** tends to imply a deviation from some standard form of language, usually the dialect used by educated upper-class or upper-middle-class people, known in English as 'standard' English.

Dialects may be regional in nature. Thus in Britain there is a Cornish dialect, a Liverpool dialect, a Glasgow dialect, and so on. Alternatively, they may be based on class differences, when they are sometimes known as 'social dialects'. These include working-class dialect, upper-class dialect, and so on.

At one time regional dialects were looked down on by

60

people who spoke only standard English. People with regional accents, using regional dialects, were unlikely to get jobs in professions such as radio and television, where the use of language was a major consideration. People intent on such careers tried to change their accents to remove all traces of dialect. However, things have changed, and now it is quite common for people using regional accents and dialects to have jobs associated with radio and television.

Note that the word **dialect** is not appropriate if it is a global variety of English that is being referred to. For example, the English spoken in America is known as American English.

diction has two meanings. It can refer to the choice of words in writing or speech, especially with regard to correctness, clarity or effectiveness, as in 'The content of his essay was very interesting but his diction was poor'. It can also refer to the pronunciation and enunciation of words in speaking and singing, as in 'She has a beautiful natural singing voice but should take lessons in diction'.

dialogue in novels, etc, is placed on a new line, often in a new paragraph, if there is a change of speaker, as in:

'We're going now', said John. 'Do you want to join us? If you do you'd better hurry. We can't wait.'

'Just go on', replied Mary. 'I'm not quite ready. I'll catch you up'.

digraph refers to a group of two letters representing one sound, as in 'ay' in 'hay', 'ey' in 'key', 'oy' in 'boy', 'ph' in 'phone' and 'th' in 'thin'. When the **digraph** consists of two letters physically joined together as 'ae', it is called a 'ligature'.

diminutive refers to something small or a small form or version of something, as in 'booklet', 'droplet', 'flatlet', 'auntie', 'doggy', 'islet', 'piglet', 'poppet', 'snippet', 'starlet', 'kitchenette', 'hillock', 'paddock', 'mannikin', 'lambkin', 'duckling', 'gosling', 'nestling', 'majorette', 'pipette'. Proper names often have diminutive forms. as in 'Alf' for Alfred, 'Annie' for Ann, 'Babs' for Barbara, 'Bill' for William, 'Charlie' for Charles, 'Dot' for Dorothy, 'Jimmy' for James, 'Lizzie' for Elizabeth, 'Meg' for Margaret, 'Nell' for Helen, 'Pat' for Patrick and 'Teddy' for Edward.

diphthong is a speech sound that changes its quality within the same single syllable. The sound begins as for one vowel and moves on as for another. Since the sound glides from one vowel into another, a **diphthong** is sometimes called a 'gliding vowel'. Examples include the vowels sounds in 'rain', 'weigh', 'either', 'voice', 'height', 'aisle', 'road', 'soul', 'know', 'house', 'care', 'pure', 'during', 'here' and 'weird'.

direct object refers to the noun, noun phrase, noun or nominal clause or pronoun which is acted upon by the action of a transitive verb. In the sentence 'She bought milk', 'bought' is a transitive verb and 'milk' is a noun which is the direct object. In the sentence 'She bought loads of clothes', 'bought' is a transitive verb and 'loads of clothes' is the direct object. In the sentence 'He knows what happened', 'knows' is a transitive verb and 'what happened' is a 'noun clause' or 'nominal clause'. A **direct object** is frequently known just as 'object'. *See* IN-DIRECT OBJECT.

direct speech refers to the reporting of speech by repeating exactly the actual words used by the speaker. In the sentence 'Peter said, "I am tired of this"', "I am tired of this" is a piece of direct speech because it represents exactly what Peter said. Similarly, in the sentence 'Jane asked, "Where are you going?"', "Where are you going" is a piece of direct speech since it represents exactly what Jane said.

Quotation marks, also known as inverted commas or informally as quotes, are used at the beginning and the end of pieces of **direct speech.** Only the words actually spoken are placed within the quotation marks, as in '"If I were you," he said, "I would refuse to go"'. The quotation marks involved can be either single or double, according to preference or house style.

If there is a statement such as 'he said' following the piece of direct speech, a comma is placed before the second inverted comma, as in '"Come along," he said'. If the piece of direct speech is a question or exclamation, a question mark or exclamation mark is put instead of the comma, as in '"What are you doing?" asked John' and '"Get away from me!" she screamed'.

If a statement such as 'he said' is placed within a sentence in direct speech, a comma is placed after 'he said' and the second part of the piece of direct speech does not begin with a capital letter, as in "'I know very well," he said, "that you do not like me.'"

If the piece of direct speech includes a complete sentence, the sentence begins with a capital letter, as in "'I am going away," she said, "and I am not coming back. I don't feel that I belong here anymore.'" Note that the full stop at the end of a piece of direct speech that is a sentence should go before the closing inverted comma.

If the piece of direct speech quoted takes up more than one paragraph, quotation marks are placed at the beginning of each new paragraph. However, quotation marks are not placed at the end of each paragraph, just at the end of the final one.

When writing a story, etc, which includes dialogue or conversation, each new piece of direct speech should begin on a new line or sometimes in a new paragraph.

Quotation marks are not used only to indicate **direct speech.** For example, they are sometimes used to indicate the title of a book or newspaper. The quotation marks used in this way can be either single or double, according to preference or house style. If a piece of direct speech contains the title of a book, newspaper, etc, it should be put in the opposite type of quotation marks to those used to enclose the piece of direct speech. Thus, if single quotation marks have been used in the direct speech, then double quotation marks should be used for the title within the direct speech, as in "Have you read "Animal Farm" by George Orwell?' the teacher asked'. If double quotation marks have been used for the direct speech, single quotation marks should be used for the title, as in '"Have you read 'Animal Farm?' by George Orwell?" the teacher asked'.

Sometimes titles are put in italic type instead of quotation marks. This avoids the clumsiness which can occur when both sets of quotation marks end on the same word, as in 'The pupil replied, 'No, I have not read "Animal Farm".''

dis- is a prefix derived from Latin indicating 'opposite', 'not', as in 'disappear', 'disapprove', 'disband', 'disbelieve', 'disclaim', 'disconnect', 'discontinue', 'disenchant', 'disengage', 'disinherit', 'dislike', 'disobey', 'dispossess', 'distrust', and 'disunite'.

distributive pronouns refer to individual members of a class or group. These include 'each', 'either', 'neither', 'none', 'everyone', 'no one'. Such pronouns, where relevant, should be accompanied by singular verbs and singular personal pronouns, as in 'All the men are to be considered for the new posts. Each is to send in his application'. Problems arise when the sex of the noun to which the **distributive pronoun** refers back is either unknown or unspecified. Formerly it was the convention to treat such nouns as masculine and so to make the **distributive pronoun** masculine, as in 'All pupils must obey the rules. Each is to provide his own sports equipment'. Nowadays this convention is frequently considered to be unacceptably sexist and attempts have been made to get round this. One solution is to use 'him/her' (or 'him or her'), etc, as in 'The students have received

a directive from the professor. Each is to produce his/
her essay by tomorrow.' This convention is considered
by many people to be clumsy. They prefer to be
ungrammatical and use a plural personal pronoun, as in
'The pupils are being punished. Each is to inform their
parents'. Where possible it is preferable to rephrase sentences to avoid being either sexist or ungrammatical, as
in 'All of the pupils must tell their parents.'

Each, either, etc, in such contexts is fairly formal. In
less formal situations 'each of', 'either of', etc, is more
usual, as in 'Each of the boys will have to train really
hard to win' and 'Either of the dresses is perfectly suitable'.

disyllabic means having two syllable. For example 'window' is disyllabic, since it consists of the syllable 'win'
and the syllable 'dow'. Similarly 'curtain' is disyllabic
since it consists of the syllable 'cur' and 'tain'.

do is an auxiliary verb which is used to form negative
forms, as in, 'I do not agree with you', 'They do not
always win', 'He does not wish to go' and 'She did not
approve of their behaviour'. It is also used to form interrogative forms, as in 'Do you agree?', 'Does she know
about it?', 'Did you see that?' and 'I prefer to go by
train. Don't you?' **Do** is also used for emphasis, as in 'I
do believe you're right' and 'They do know, don't they?'

-dom is a suffix meaning 'state, condition', as in 'bore-
dom', 'freedom', 'officialdom', 'martyrdom'. It can also
mean 'rank or status', as in 'earldom', 'dukedom', or
'domain, territory' as in 'kingdom'.

double negative refers to the occurrence of two negative words in a single sentence or clause, as in 'He didn't say nothing' and 'We never had no quarrel'. This is usually considered incorrect in standard English, although it is a feature of some social or regional dialects. The use of the **double negative**, if taken literally, often has the opposite meaning to the one intended. Thus 'He didn't say nothing' conveys the idea that 'He said something'.

Some **double negatives** are considered acceptable, as in 'I wouldn't be surprised if they don't turn up', although it is better to restrict such constructions to informal contexts. The sentence quoted conveys the impression that the speaker will be quite surprised if 'they' do 'turn up'. Another example of an acceptable **double negative** is 'I can't not worry about the children. Anything could have happened to them'. Again this type of construction is best restricted to informal contexts.

It is the semi-negative forms, such as 'hardly' and 'scarcely', which cause most problems with regard to **double negatives**, as in 'We didn't have hardly any money to buy food' and 'They didn't have barely enough time to catch the bus'. Such sentences are incorrect.

double passive refers to a clause which contains two verbs in the passive, the second of which is an infinitive, as in 'The goods are expected to be despatched some time this week'. Some examples of **double passives** are clumsy or ungrammatical and should be avoided, as in 'Redundancy notices are proposed to be issued next week'.

doubling of consonants causes spelling problems. There are a few rules which help to solve these problems. These include the following: In words of one syllable ending in a single consonant preceded by a single vowel, the consonant is doubled when an ending starting with a vowel is added, as in 'drop' and 'dropped', 'pat' and 'patting' and 'rub' and 'rubbing'.

In words of more than one syllable that end in a single consonant preceded by a single vowel, the consonant is doubled if the stress is on the last syllable, as in 'begin' and 'beginning', 'occur' and 'occurring', 'prefer' and 'preferred', 'refer' and 'referring' and 'commit' and 'committed'. In similar words where the stress is not on the last syllable, the consonant does not double, as in 'bigot' and 'bigoted' and 'develop' and 'developed'.

Exceptions to this rule include words ending in 'l'. The 'l' doubles even in cases where the last syllable containing it is unstressed, as in 'travel' and 'travelled' and 'appal' and 'appalling'. 'Worship', in which the stress is on the first syllable, is also an exception, as in 'worshipped'.

doubles are words that habitually go together, as in 'out and out', 'neck and neck', 'over and over', 'hale and hearty', 'rant and rave', 'fast and furious', 'hue and cry', 'stuff and nonsense', 'rough and ready', 'might and main', 'give and take', 'ups and downs', 'fair and square', 'high and dry' and 'wear and tear'. **Doubles** are also sometimes called **dyads**.

doublets are pairs of words that have developed from the same original word but now differ somewhat in form and usually in meaning. Examples include 'human' and 'humane', 'shade' and 'shadow', 'hostel' and 'hotel', 'frail' and 'fragile', and 'fashion' and 'faction'.

dramatic irony refers to a situation in which a character in a play, novel, etc, says or does something that has a meaning for the audience or reader, other than the obvious meaning, that he/she does not understand. Its use is common in both comedy and tragedy.

dual gender refers to a category of nouns in which there is no indication of gender. The nouns referred to include a range of words used for people, and occasionally animals, which can be of either gender. Unless the gender is specified we do not know the sex of the person referred to. Such words include 'artist', 'author', 'poet', 'singer', 'child', 'pupil', 'student', 'baby', 'parent', 'teacher', 'dog'. Such words give rise to problems with accompanying singular pronouns. *See* EACH.

dummy subject describes a subject that has no intrinsic meaning but is inserted to maintain a balanced grammatical structure. In the sentences 'It has started to rain' and 'It is nearly midnight', 'it' is a dummy subject. In the sentences 'There is nothing else to say' and 'There is no reason for his behaviour', 'there' is a dummy subject.

dyads see **doubles**.

dynamic verb refers to a verb with a meaning that indicates action, as 'work' in 'They work hard', 'play' in 'The boys play football at the weekend' and 'come' in 'The girls come here every Sunday'.

dys-

dys- is a prefix derived from the Greek meaning 'bad', as in 'dyslexia', 'dysgraphia', 'dysmenorrhea', 'dyspepsia'.

E

each can be either a DETERMINER or a DISTRIBUTIVE PRONOUN.
Each as a determiner is used before a singular noun and
is accompanied by a singular verb, as in 'Each candidate is to reapply', 'Each athlete has a place in the final', 'Each country is represented by a head of state'
and 'Each chair was covered in chintz'.

Each of can sometimes be used instead of **each**, as in
'each of the candidates'. Again a singular verb is used,
as in 'Each of the books has pages missing', 'Each of
the chairs has a broken leg' and 'Each of the pupils is to
make a contribution to the cost of the outing'. **Each of**
can also be used in front of plural pronouns, as in 'each
of them'. Once again a singular verb is used, as in 'Each
of them wants something different', 'Each of us is supposed to make a contribution' and 'Each of the words
has several meanings'. If the user wishes to emphasize
the fact that something is true about every member of a
group, **each one of** should be used and not 'every', as in
'Each one of them feels guilty', 'Each one of us has a
part to play' and 'Each one of the actors has improved'.

As a pronoun **each** also takes a singular verb, as in
'They hate each other. Each is plotting revenge', 'These

71

exercises are not a waste of time. Each provides valuable experience'. For emphasis **each one** can be used, as in 'We cannot leave any of these books behind. Each one of them is necessary' and 'We should not dismiss any of the staff. Each one has a part to play in the new firm'.

Each, where relevant, should be accompanied by a singular personal pronoun, as in 'Each girl has to provide her own sports equipment', 'Each of the men is to take a turn at working night shift', 'The boys are all well off and each can afford the cost of the holiday' and 'There are to be no exceptions among the women staff. Each one has to work full time'.

Problems arise when the noun that **each** refers back to is of unknown or unspecified sex. Formerly nouns in such situations were assumed to be masculine, as in 'Each pupil was required to bring his own tennis racket' and 'Each of the students has to provide himself with a tape recorder'. Nowadays such a convention is regarded as being sexist and the use of 'he/her', 'his/her', etc, is proposed, as in 'Each pupil was required to bring his/her (or 'his or her') own tennis racket' and 'Each student has to provide himself/herself (or 'himself or herself') with a tape recorder'. Even in written English such a convention can be clumsy and it is even more so in spoken English. For this reason many people decide to be ungrammatical and opt for 'Each pupil was required to bring their own tennis racket' and 'Each student has to provide themselves with a tape recorder'.

Both sexism and grammatical error can be avoided by rephrasing such sentences, as in 'All pupils are required to bring their own tennis rackets' and 'All students have to provide themselves with tape recorders'.

Each is used rather than **every** when the user is thinking of the members of a group as individuals.

eco- is a prefix indicating ecology. Following the increased awareness of the importance of the environment, there has been a growing interest in ecology and many words beginning with **eco-** have been added to the English language. Some of these are scientific terms such as 'ecotype', 'ecosystem' or 'ecospecies'. Others are more general terms, such as 'ecocatastrophe' and 'ecopolitics', and some are even slang terms, such as 'ecofreak' and 'econut'.

-ectomy is a suffix of Greek origin which indicates 'surgical removal', as in 'hysterectomy', the surgical removal of the womb, 'mastectomy', the surgical removal of a breast, and 'appendicectomy', the surgical removal of the appendix, the American English version of which is 'appendectomy'.

-ed is a suffix which forms the past tense and past participles of regular verbs, as in 'asked', 'blinded', 'caused', 'darkened', 'escaped', 'frightened', 'guarded', 'hunted', 'injured', 'jilted', 'kicked', 'landed', 'marked', 'noted', 'opened', 'painted', 'quarrelled', 'rattled', 'started', 'tormented', 'unveiled', 'washed', 'yielded'. Some past participles ending in '-ed' can act as adjectives, as in 'darkened room', 'escaped prisoners', 'frightened children', 'hunted animals', 'painted faces' and 'tormented souls'.

In the case of some verbs, the past tense and past participle may end in '-ed' or 't', according to preference. Such verbs include 'burn', 'dream', 'dwell', 'kneel', 'lean', 'leapt', 'smell', 'spell', 'spill' and 'spoil'. Thus 'burned' and 'burnt', 'dreamed' and 'dreamt', 'kneeled' and 'knelt', and 'learned' and 'learnt', etc, are acceptable forms.

-ee is a suffix derived from French and is used as part of nouns that are the recipients of an action, as in 'deportee', a person who has been deported; 'employee', a person who is employed; 'interviewee', a person who is being interviewed; 'licensee', a person who has been licensed; 'trainee', a person who is being trained.

-Ee can also be used as part of a noun indicating a person who acts or behaves in a particular way, as 'absentee', a person who absents himself/herself and 'escapee', a person who escapes.

e.g. is the abbreviation of the Latin phrase *exempli gratia* and means 'for example'. It is used before examples of what has previously been referred to, as in 'The tourists want to visit the historic sites of Edinburgh, e.g. Edinburgh Castle and Holyrood House'. By its very nature e.g. is mostly restricted to written English, becoming 'for example' in speech. Many writers also prefer to use 'for example' rather than use e.g. Both letters of the abbreviation usually have a full stop after them, as e.g., and it is usually preceded by a comma.

either can be used as either a determiner or distributive pronoun. As a determiner it is used with a singular verb, as in 'Either hotel is expensive' and 'In principle they are both against the plan but is either likely to vote for it?'

Either of can be used instead of **either**. It is used before a plural noun, as in 'either of the applicants' and 'either of the houses'. It is accompanied by a singular verb, as in 'Either of the applicants is suitable' and 'Either of the houses is big enough for their family'.

Either can be used as a distributive pronoun and takes a singular verb, as in 'We have looked at both houses and either is suitable' and 'She cannot decide between the two dresses but either is appropriate for the occasion'. This use is rather formal.

In the **either .... or** construction, a singular verb is used if both subjects are singular, as in 'Either Mary or Jane knows what to do' and 'Either my mother or my father plans to be present'. A plural verb is used if both nouns involved are plural, as in 'Either men or women can play' and 'Either houses or flats are available'.

When a combination of singular and plural subjects is involved, the verb traditionally agrees with the subject which is nearer to it, as in 'Either his parents or his sister is going to come' and 'Either his grandmother or his parents are going to come'.

As a pronoun, **either** should be used only of two possibilities.

electro- is a prefix meaning 'electric, electrical' as in 'electrocardiograph', 'electromagnetic', 'electroscope', 'electrotherapy'.

elision refers to the omission of a speech sound or syllable, as in the omission of 'd' in one of the possible pro-
nunciations of 'Wednesday' and in the omission of 'ce'
from the pronunciation of 'Gloucester'.

ellipsis indicates omission of some kind. It can refer to
the omission of words from a statement because they
are thought to be obvious from the context. In many cases
it involves using an auxiliary verb on its own rather than
a full verb, as in 'Jane won't accept it but Mary will' and
'They would go if they could'. In such cases the full
form of 'Jane won't accept it but Mary will accept it'
and 'They would go if they could go' would sound un-
natural and repetitive. This is common in spoken English. Some sentences containing an ellipsis sound clumsy
as well as ungrammatical, as in 'This is as good, or perhaps even better than that', where 'as' is omittedafter
'good' and in 'People have and still do express their disapproval about it', where 'expressed' is omitted after
'have'. Care should be taken to avoid ellipsis if the use
of it is going to be ambiguous or clumsy.

Ellipsis is often used to indicate an omission from a
quoted passage. If part of a passage is quoted and there
is a gap before the next piece of the same passage is
required to be quoted an **ellipsis** is used in the form of
three dots. If the part of the passage quoted does not
start at the beginning of a sentence the ellipsis precedes
it.

emphasizing adjective is an adjective used for emphasis.

'Very' is an **emphasizing adjective** in the sentence 'His very mother dislikes him' and 'own' is an **emphasizing adjective** in 'He likes to think that he is own master'.

emphasizing adverb is an adverb used for emphasis. 'Really' is an **emphasizing adverb** in the sentence 'She really doesn't care whether she lives or dies' and 'positively' is an **emphasizing adverb** in the sentence 'He positively does not want to know anything about it'.

emphatic pronoun is a reflexive pronoun that is used for emphasis, as in 'He knows himself that he is wrong', 'She admitted herself that she had made a mistake' and 'The teachers themselves say that the headmaster is too strict'.

-en is a suffix with several functions. In one sense it indicates 'causing to be', as in 'broaden', 'darken', 'gladden', 'lighten' and 'sweeten'. It also indicates a diminutive or small version of something, as in 'chicken' and 'maiden'. It also indicates what something is made of, as in 'silken', 'wooden' and 'woollen'. It is also used to form the past participle of many irregular words, as 'broken', 'fallen', 'forgotten' and 'taken'.

en- is a prefix indicating 'causing to be', as in 'enrich' and 'enlarge', and 'putting into', as in 'endanger', 'enrage', 'enslave'.

ending is the final part of a word consisting of an inflection which is added to a base or root word. The '-ren' part of 'children' is an ending, the '-er' of 'poorer' is an ending and the '-ing' of 'falling' is an ending.

epic originally referred to a very long narrative poem dealing with heroic deeds and adventures on a grand scale, as Homer's 'Iliad'. In modern usage it has been extended to include novels or films with some of these qualities.

epigram is a figure of speech consisting of a brief, pointed and witty saying, as in Jonathan Swift's 'Every man desires to live long; but no man would be old' and Oscar Wilde's 'A cynic is a man who knows the price of everything and the value of nothing'. **Epigram** originally referred to a short poem inscribed on a public monument or tomb.

epithet is an adjective that describes a quality of a noun, as in 'a beautiful dress', 'an amazing story' and 'an enjoyable occasion'. It is also used to indicate a term of abuse, as in 'The drunk man let out a stream of epithets at the policeman.'

eponym refers to a person after whom something is named. The name of the thing in question can also be referred to as an eponym, or it can be said to be eponymous, eponymous being the adjective from **eponym**. English has several eponymous words. Some of these are listed below together with their derivations.

Bailey bridge, a type of temporary military bridge that can be assembled very quickly, called after Sir Donald **Bailey** (1901-85), the English engineer who invented it.

Bowie knife, a type of hunting knife with a long curving blade, called after the American soldier and adventurer, James **Bowie** (1799-1836), who made it popular.

cardigan, a knitted jacket fastened with buttons called after the Earl of **Cardigan** (1797-1868) who was fond of wearing such a garment and was the British cavalry officer who led the unsuccessful Charge of the Light Brigade during the Crimean War (1854).

Celsius the temperature scale, called after the Swedish astronomer, Anders **Celsius** (1701-44).

freesia, a type of sweet-smelling flower, called after the German physician, Friedrich Heinrich Theodor **Freese** (died 1876).

garibaldi, a type of biscuit with a layer of currants in it, called after Giuseppe **Garibaldi** (1807-1882), an Italian soldier patriot who is said to have enjoyed such biscuits.

Granny Smith, a variety of hard green apple, called after the Australian gardener, Maria Ann Smith, known as **Granny Smith** (died 1870), who first grew the apple in Sydney in the 1860s.

greengage, a type of greenish plum, called after Sir William **Gage** who introduced it into Britain from France (1777-1864).

leotard, a one-piece, close-fitting garment worn by acrobats and dancers, called after the French acrobat, Jules **Leotard** (1842-70), who introduced the costume as a circus garment.

mackintosh, a type of raincoat, especially one made of rubberized cloth, called after the Scottish chemist, Charles **Mackintosh** (1766-1843), who patented it in the early 1820s.

praline, a type of confectionery made from nuts and sugar, is called after Count Plessis-**Praslin** (1598-1675), a French field marshal, whose chef is said to have been the first person to make the sweet.

plimsoll, a type of light rubber-soled canvas shoe, called after the English shipping reform leader, Samuel **Plimsoll** (1824-98). The shoe is so named because the upper edge of the rubber was thought to resemble the **Plimsoll** Line, the set of markings on the side of a ship which indicate the levels to which the ship may be safely loaded. The Plimsoll Line became law in 1876.

salmonella, the bacteria that causes some diseases such as food poisoning, called after Daniel Elmer **Salmon** (1850-1914), the American veterinary surgeon who identified it.

sandwich, a snack consisting of two pieces of buttered bread with a filling, called after the Earl of **Sandwich** (1718-92) who was such a compulsive gambler that he would not leave the gaming tables to eat, but had some cold beef between two slices of bread brought to him.

saxophone, a type of keyed brass instrument often used in jazz music, called after Adolphe **Sax** (1814-94), the Belgium instrument-maker who invented it.

shrapnel, an explosive projectile that contains bullets or fragments of metal and a charge that is exploded before impact, called after the British army officer, Henry **Shrapnel** (1761–1842), who invented it.

stetson, a type of wide-brimmed, high-crowned felt hat, called after its designer, the American hat-maker, John Batterson **Stetson** (1830-1906).

trilby, a type of soft felt hat with an indented crown, called after 'Trilby', the dramatized version of the novel by the English writer, George du Maurier. The heroine of the play, Trilby O'Ferrall, wore such a hat.

wellington, a waterproof rubber boot that extends to the knee, called after the Duke of **Wellington** (1769-1852), who defeated Napoleon at Waterloo (1815).

equative indicates that one thing is equal to, or the same as, another. The verb 'to be' is sometimes known as an **equative verb** because it links a subject and complement which are equal to each other, as in 'He is a rogue' ('he' and 'rogue' refer to the same person) and 'His wife is a journalist' ('his wife' and 'journalist' refer to the same person). Other **equative verbs** include 'appear', 'become', 'look', 'remain' and 'seem', as in 'She looks a nasty person' and 'He became a rich man'. Such verbs are more usually known as **copular verbs**.

-er is a suffix with several functions. It can indicate 'a person that does something', as in 'bearer', 'cleaner', 'employer', 'farmer', 'manager'. Some words in this category can also end in '-or', as in 'adviser/advisor'. It can also indicate 'a person who is engaged in something', as in 'lawyer'. It also indicates 'a thing which does something', as in 'blender', 'cooker', 'mower', 'printer' and 'strainer'. It can also indicate the comparative form of an adjective, as in 'darker', 'fairer', 'older', 'shorter' and 'younger'. It can also indicate 'someone that comes from somewhere', as in 'Londoner' and 'Southerner'.

-esque is a prefix of French origin which means 'in the style or fashion of', as in 'Junoesque', 'statuesque', 'Picassoesque', 'Ramboesque'.

-ese is a suffix indicating 'belonging to, coming from' and is used of people and languages, as 'Chinese', 'Japanese' and 'Portuguese'. By extension it refers to words indicating some kind of jargon, as 'computerese', 'journalese' and 'officialese'.

Esq. can be used instead of 'Mr' when addressing an envelope to a man, as in 'John Jones, Esq.'. It is mostly used in formal contexts. Note that Esq. is used instead of 'Mr', not as well as it. It is usually spelt with a full stop.

-ess is a suffix which was formerly widely used to indicate the feminine form of a word, as 'authoress' from 'author', 'poetess' from 'poet', 'editress' from 'editor', and 'sculptress' from 'sculptor'. In many cases the supposed male form, such as 'author', is now considered a neutral form and so is used of both a woman and a man. Thus a woman as well as a man may be an author, a poet, an editor and a sculptor, etc. Some words ending in **-ess** remain, as princess, duchess, heiress and hostess. Actress and waitress are still also fairly widespread.

-est is a suffix which indicates the superlative forms of adjectives, as in 'biggest', 'hardest', 'lowest', 'smallest', 'ugliest'.

etc is the abbreviation of a Latin phrase *et cetera*, meaning 'and the rest, and other things'. It is used at the end of lists to indicate that there exist other examples of the kind of thing that has just been named, as in 'He grows potatoes, carrots, turnips, etc', 'The girls can play tennis, hockey, squash, etc', 'The main branch of the bank can supply francs, marks, lire, kroner, etc'. **Etc** is preceded by a comma and is also spelt with a full stop.

-ette is a suffix indicating a diminutive or smaller version, as 'cigarette', 'kitchenette', 'rosette', 'serviette'. It can also indicate 'imitation', as in 'flannelette', 'leatherette', 'satinette'. It can also indicate 'female', as in 'majorette', 'usherette', 'suffragette'. In this last sense it is sometimes used disparagingly, as in 'jockette' (a derogatory word for a female jockey) and 'hackette' (a derogatory word for a female journalist).

etymology refers to the source of the formation of a word and the development of its meaning, as in 'What is the etymology of the word "biochemistry"?' It also means the branch of language studies that deals with the origin and development of words, as in 'He specializes in etymology'. In addition it refers to an account or statement of the formation of a word or phrase, as in 'Does that dictionary have etymologies?' In larger dictionaries it is usual to include etymologies, often at the end of each entry. These indicate which language the relevant word has been derived from, for example, whether it has come from Old English, Norse, Latin, Greek, French, German, Dutch, Italian, Spanish, etc. Alternatively they indicate which person, place, etc, the word has been named after. Some dictionaries also include the date at which the relevant word entered the English language. *See* BORROWING.

Many words and phrases in the English language are of unknown or uncertain origin. In such cases much guesswork goes on and various suggestions put forward, most of which cannot be proved.

euphemism is a term given to an expression that is a milder, more pleasant, less direct way of saying something that might be thought to be too harsh or direct. English has a great many euphemisms, many of these referring to certain areas of life. Euphemisms range from the high-flown, to the coy, to slang. Some examples of euphemisms and of the areas in which they tend to occur are listed below.

euphemisms for 'die' or 'be dead':

'be in the arms of Jesus', 'be laid to rest', 'be with one's maker', 'be no longer with us', 'be with the Lord', 'be written out of the script', 'bite the dust', 'cash in one's chips', 'croak', 'depart this life', 'go to a better place', 'go the way of all flesh', 'go to one's long home', 'go to the happy hunting grounds', 'have been taken by the grim reaper', 'have bought it', 'have breathed one's last', 'have gone to a better place', 'kick the bucket', 'meet one's end', 'pass away', 'pay the supreme sacrifice', 'pop off', 'push up the daisies', 'rest in peace', 'shuffle off this mortal coil', 'slip one's rope', 'turn up one's toes'.

euphemisms for 'old':

'getting on a bit', 'not as young as one was', 'not in the first flush of youth', 'in the sunset years', 'in the twilight years', 'of advanced years', 'so many years young (as in 90 years young)'.

euphemisms for 'suicide':

'do away with one self', 'die by one's own hand', 'end

it all', 'make away with oneself', 'take one's own life', 'take the easy way out', 'top oneself'.

euphemisms for 'to dismiss':
'declare (someone) redundant', 'deselect', 'dispense with (someone's) services', 'give early retirement to', 'give (someone) a golden handshake', 'give (someone) his/ her marching orders', 'let (someone) go', 'not to renew (someone's) contract'.

euphemisms for 'drunk':
'blotto', 'feeling no pain', 'happy', 'half-cut', 'legless', 'merry', 'one over the eight', 'plastered', 'three sheets to the wind', 'tiddly', 'tipsy', 'tired and emotional', 'squiffy', 'well-oiled'.

euphemisms for 'naked':
'in a state of nature', 'in one's birthday suit', 'in the buff', 'in the nuddy', 'in the raw', 'starkers', 'without a stitch', 'wearing only a smile'.

euphemisms for 'pregnant':
'awaiting the patter of tiny feet', 'expecting', 'expecting a happy event', 'in a delicate condition', 'in an interesting condition', 'in the club', 'in the family way', 'in the pudding club', 'up the pole', 'up the spout', 'with a bun in the oven'.

euphemisms for 'to have sexual intercourse':
'be intimate with', 'do it', 'get one's end away', 'go to bed with', 'have it off with', 'make love', 'make out', 'sleep with', 'score'.

euphemisms for 'sexual intercourse':
'hanky panky', 'intimacy', 'nookie', 'roll in the hay',

'rumpy pumpy/rumpty pumpty'.

euphemisms for to go to the toilet:

'answer the call of nature', 'freshen up', 'go somewhere', 'pay a visit', 'powder one's nose', 'spend a penny', 'take a slash', 'wash one's hands'.

euphemisms for 'toilet':

'bathroom', 'bog', 'can', 'john', 'karzy', 'powder room', 'rest room', 'the facilities', 'the conveniences', 'the geography of the house', 'the little boys' room/the little girls' room', 'the littlest room', 'the smallest room', 'the plumbing', 'wash room'.

euphemisms and political correctness:

Many of the expressions advocated by the politically correct movement for viewing physical and mental disabilities in a more positive light are in fact **euphemisms**. These include 'aurally challenged' for 'deaf', 'optically challenged' for 'blind', and 'uniquely abled' for 'physically disabled'.

Euro-is a prefix meaning either 'referring to Europe', as in 'Eurovision', but more commonly now 'referring to the European Community', as in 'Euro-MP', 'Eurocrat', 'Eurocurrency'.

every is used with a singular noun to indicate that all the members of a group are being referred to. It takes a singular verb, as in 'Every soldier must report for duty', 'Every machine is to be inspected' and 'Every house has a different view'. **Every** should also be accompanied, where relevant, by a singular pronoun, as in 'Every boy has his job to do', 'Every girl is to wear a dress' and

'Every machine is to be replaced'. Problems arise when the sex of the noun to which **every** refers is unknown or unspecified. Formerly it was the custom to assume such a noun to be masculine and to use masculine pronouns, as in 'Every pupil is to behave himself properly. This assumption is now regarded as sexist, and to avoid this 'he/she', 'him/her' and 'his/her' can be used. Many people feel that this convention can become clumsy and prefer to be ungrammatical by using 'they', 'them' and 'their', as in 'Every pupil is to behave themselves properly.' Many sentences of this kind can be rephrased to avoid being either sexist or ungrammatical, as in 'All pupils are to behave themselves properly'. *See* EACH.

everyone is a pronoun which takes a singular verb, as in 'Everyone is welcome' and 'Everyone has the right to a decent standard of living'. In order to be grammatically correct, it should be accompanied, where relevant, by a singular personal pronoun but it is subject to the same kind of treatment as **every**. *See* EVERY.

ex- is a prefix meaning 'former', as in 'ex-chairman', 'ex-president', 'ex-wife'.

exclamation is a word, phrase or sentence called out with strong feeling of some kind. It is marked by an **exclamation mark** which occurs at the end of the **exclamation**, as in 'Get lost!', 'What a nerve!', 'Help!', 'Ouch!' 'Well I never!', 'What a disaster!', 'I'm tired of all this!' and 'Let me out of here!' An **exclamatory question** is a sentence that is interrogative in form but is an **exclamation** in meaning, as in 'Isn't the baby beautiful!' and

extra-

'Isn't it lovely!'.

extra-is a prefix meaning 'beyond, outside' as in 'extra-marital', 'extra-terrestrial', 'extra-curricular'.

F

fable is a story that is intended to convey a moral lesson. Fables frequently feature animals which speak and act like human beings. Most famous are those of Aesop, a Phrygian slave (620–560 BC), who wrote such fables as 'The Hare and the Tortoise' and 'The Fox and the Grapes'.

false friends refer to words that have the same or similar forms in different languages but have different meanings in each. For example, the French word *abusif* and the English word 'abusive' are **false friends**. *Abusif* does not mean 'abusive' but 'incorrect, illegal, unauthorized, excessive'. Similarly, the French word *actuel* and the English 'actual' are **false friends**. *Actuel* does not mean 'actual' but 'present-day'. Similarly, the French *eventuel* and Italian *eventuale* are false freinds with the English 'eventual'. *Eventuel* and *eventuale* do not mean 'eventual' but 'possible', while *sensible* in French and *sensibile* in Italian do not mean 'sensible, having good sense or judgement' but 'sensitive, tender, touchy'.

feminine refers to the gender that indicates female persons or animals. It is the opposite of 'masculine'. The feminine gender demands the use of the appropriate pronoun, including 'she', 'her', 'hers' and 'herself', as in 'The girl tried to save the dog but *she* was unable to do so', 'The woman hurt *her* leg', 'Mary said that the book is *hers*', and 'The waitress cut *herself*'.

feminine forms of words, formed by adding —*ess*, used to be common but many such forms are now thought to be sexist. Words such as 'author', 'sculptor', 'poet' are now considered to be neutral terms that can be used to refer to a man or a woman. Some *-ess* words are either still being used or are in a state of flux, as in 'actress'. See -ESS.

few and **a few** are not interchangeable. Both expressions mean 'some, but not many', but they convey different impressions. **Few** is the opposite of 'many', as in 'We have few resources' and 'We have few ideas left'. **A few** conveys a more positive impression and is the opposite of 'none', as in 'We have a few pounds set aside for Christmas' and 'We have not reached a definite decision but we have a few ideas in hand'. The sentence 'We have few ideas left' indicates a negative situation, that 'we' are running out of 'ideas', but the sentence 'We have a few ideas in hand' conveys a positive impression.

fewer and **less** are liable to be used wrongly. **Fewer** means 'a smaller number of' and should be used with plural nouns, as in 'fewer problems', 'fewer resources', 'fewer fears', 'fewer boxes', 'fewer books', 'fewer bottles' and 'fewer chairs'. **Less** means 'a smaller amount of' and should be used with singular nouns, as in 'less responsibility', less anxiety', less work', 'less milk', 'less wood' and 'less material'. It is a very common error to use **less** where **fewer** is correct, as in 'less bottles' and 'less queues'.

figurative refers to words that are not used literally. For example, 'mine' in the sense of 'excavation in the earth from which coal, tin, etc, is taken' is a literal use of the word. 'Mine' in the sense of 'He is a mine of information' is a figurative use of the word. There are many figurative expressions in English. These include 'take the bull by the horns', 'put one's shoulder to the wheel', 'hide one's light under a bushel', 'be in seventh heaven', 'count one's chickens', 'change horses in mid-stream', 'blow hot and cold', 'run with the hare and hunt with the hounds', 'make the feathers fly', 'put the cat among the pigeons', 'cut corners', 'cry over spilt milk', 'jump on the bandwagon', 'let the grass grow under one's feet', 'drop a brick', 'burn the midnight oil', 'show a clean pair of heels', 'turn one's coat', 'drive a coach and horses through' and 'take coals to Newcastle'.

figure of speech is a form of expression used to heighten the effect of a statement. The most commonly known are 'similes' and 'metaphors' but there are many more, such as 'personification'. See the individual entries for further information.

finite verb is a verb that has a tense and has a subject with which it agrees in number and person. For example 'cries' is finite in the sentence 'The child cries most of the time', and 'looks' is finite in the sentence 'The old man looks ill'. However 'go' in the sentence 'He wants to go' is non-finite since it has no variation of tense and does not have a subject. Similarly in the sentence 'Sitting on the river-bank, he was lost in thought', 'sitting' is non-finite.

finite clause is a clause which contains a 'finite verb', as in 'when she sees him', 'after she had defeated him', and 'as they were sitting there'.

first person refers to the person who is speaking or writing when referring to himself or herself. The **first person** pronouns are 'I', 'me', 'myself' and 'mine', with the plural forms being 'we', 'us', 'ourselves' and 'ours'. Examples include 'She said, "*I* am going home"', '"*I* am going shopping," he said', '"*We* have very little money left," she said to her husband' and 'He said, "*We* shall have to leave now if we are to get there on time"'. The first person determiners are 'my' and 'our', as in 'I have forgotten to bring *my* notebook' and 'We must remember to bring *our* books home.'

fixed phrase, also called **set phrase**, refers to a phrase that has no, or virtually no, variants, as in 'from bad to worse', 'to and fro', 'hither and thither', 'horse and cart', 'this and that', 'alas and alack' and 'rough and ready'.

-fold is a suffix meaning 'times, multiplied by', as in fourfold, a hundredfold.

for- is a prefix derived from Old English with several meanings. These include 'prohibition', as in 'forbid'; 'abstention' as in 'forbear', 'forgo' and 'forswear'; 'neglect', as in 'forsake'; 'excess, intensity', as in 'forlorn';

and 'away, off, apart', as in 'forgive'.

fore- is a prefix derived from Old English meaning 'before', as in 'forecast', 'forestall', 'foretell', 'forewarn', 'foregoing' and 'forefathers'. It can also mean 'front', as in 'foreleg', 'forehead', 'forepart'.

foreign plural refers to a plural of a word in English that has retained the plural form of the foreign word from which the English word has been derived. Examples include 'phenomena' from 'phenomenon', 'crises' from 'crisis' and 'criteria' from 'criterion'. There is a modern tendency to anglicize some of the foreign plural forms. In some cases the foreign plural form and the anglicized form exist alongside each other as 'formulae/formulas', 'thesauri/thesauruses', 'radii/radiuses', 'indices/indexes' and 'bureaux/bureaus'.

foreign expressions which have been adopted into English but not 'naturalized' are sometimes written in italic type, as in *bête noire* (a fear or obsession), *rara avis* (a rarity), *en passant* (in passing), *hors de combat*, (out of the contest, disabled), *en route* (on the way), *bon mot* (witty saying), *in toto* (completely), *in flagrante delicto* (in the very act of committing an offence), *enfant terrible* (a person who causes embarrassment by indiscreet or outrageous behaviour), *en famille* (with one's family) and *inter alia* (among other things).

-form is a suffix meaning 'having the form of', as in 'cruciform', or 'having such a number of', as in 'uniform', 'multiform'.

formal refers to speech and writing that is characterized by more complicated and more difficult language and by more complicated grammatical structures. Short forms and contractions are avoided in **formal** speech and writing. *See* INFORMAL.

formula refers to set phrases that are used in certain conventions, as in 'How do you do?', 'Yours faithfully', 'Yours sincerely', 'Kind regards', 'See you later', 'Nice to see you!' and 'Many happy returns'.

form word *see* **function word**.

-free is a suffix used to form adjectives indicating 'absence of, freedom from', as in 'carefree', 'trouble-free', 'anxiety-free', 'tax-free', 'duty-free', 'additive-free', 'lead-free'.

-friendly is a modern suffix formed on analogy with 'user-friendly' to mean 'helpful to, supporting', as in 'child-friendly', 'environment-friendly' and 'ozone-friendly'.

frequentative refers to a verb which expresses frequent repetition of an action. In English the verb endings *-le* and *-el* sometimes indicate the **frequentative** form, as in 'waddle' from 'wade', 'sparkle' from 'spark', 'crackle' from 'crack' and 'dazzle' from 'daze'. The ending *-er* can also indicate the **frequentative** form, as in 'stutter', 'spatter' and 'batter'.

-ful is a suffix indicating 'the amount that fills something', as in 'bucketful', 'basinful', 'handful', 'spoonful', 'bagful' and 'pocketful'. It can also mean 'full of', as in 'beautiful', 'truthful' and 'scornful'. It can also mean 'having the qualities of', as in 'masterful' and 'apt to, able to', as in 'forgetful', 'mournful' and 'useful'.

full stop is a punctuation mark consisting of a small dot. Its principal use is to end a sentence that is not a question or an exclamation, as in 'They spent the money.', 'She is studying hard.', 'He has been declared redundant and is very upset.' and 'Because she is shy, she rarely goes to parties.'

The **full stop** is also used in decimal fractions, as in '4.5 metres', '6.3 miles' and '12.2 litres'. It can also be used in dates, as in '22.2.94', and in times, as in '3.15 tomorrow afternoon'.

In modern usage the tendency is to omit **full stops** from abbreviations. This is most true of abbreviations involving initial capital letters as in TUC, BBC, EEC and USA. In such cases full stops should definitely not be used if one or some of the initial letters do not belong to a full word. Thus, television is abbreviated to TV and educationally subnormal to ESN.

There are usually no full stops in abbreviations involving the first and letters of a word (contractions) Dr, Mr, Rd, St, but this is a matter of taste.

Abbreviations involving the first few letters of a word, as in 'Prof' (Professor) are the most likely to have full stops, as in 'Feb.' (February), but again this is now a matter of taste.

For the use of the **full stop** in direct speech *see* DIRECT SPEECH. The **full stop** can also be called **point** or **period**.

function word is a word that has very little meaning but is primarily of grammatical significance and merely performs a 'function' in a sentence. **Function words** include determiners, and prepositions, such as in, on and up. Words which are not **function words** are sometimes known as 'content words'.

Function word is also known as **form word** or **structure word**.

future tense describes actions or states that will occur at some future time. It is marked by 'will' and 'shall'. Traditionally 'shall' was used with subjects in the first person, as in 'I shall see you tomorrow' and 'We shall go there next week', and 'will' was used with subjects in the second and third person, as in 'You will find out next week', 'He will recognize her when he sees her' and 'They will be on the next train'. Formerly 'will' was used with the first person and 'shall' with the second and third person to indicate emphasis or insistence, as in 'I *will* go on my own' and 'We *will* be able to afford it'; 'You *shall* pay what you owe' and 'The children *shall* get a holiday'. In modern usage 'shall' is usually used only for emphasis or insistence, whether with the first, second or third person, except in formal contexts. Otherwise 'will' is used, as in 'I will go tomorrow', 'We will have to see', 'You will be surprised', and 'They will be on their way by now'.

The **future tense** can also be marked by 'be about to' plus the infinitive of the relevant verb or 'be going to' plus the infinitive of the relevant verb. Examples include 'We are about to leave for work', 'They are about to go on holiday', 'She is going to be late' and 'They are going to demolish the building'.

future perfect tense is formed by 'will' or 'shall' together with the 'perfect tense', as in 'They will have been married ten years next week', 'You will have finished work by this time tomorrow' and 'By the time Jane arrives here she will have been travelling non-stop for forty-eight hours'.

G

-gate is a modern suffix which is added to a noun to indicate something scandalous. Most of the words so formed are short-lived and forgotten about almost as soon as they are invented. In modern usage they are frequently used to apply to sexual scandals, but originally **-gate** was restricted to some form of political scandal. The suffix is derived from **Watergate**, and refers to a political scandal in the United States during President Richard Nixon's re-election campaign in 1972, when Republican agents were caught breaking into the headquarters of the Democratic Party in Washington, which were in a building called the Watergate Building. The uncovering of the attempts to cover up the break-in led to Richard Nixon's resignation.

gemination refers to the doubling of consonants before a suffix. *See* DOUBLING OF CONSONANTS.

gender in the English language usually refers to the natural distinctions of sex (or absence of sex) that exist, and nouns are classified according to these distinctions—masculine, feminine and neuter. Thus, 'man', 'boy', 'king', 'prince', 'emperor', 'duke', 'heir', 'son', 'brother', 'father', 'nephew', 'husband', 'bridegroom', 'widower', 'hero', 'cock', 'drake', 'fox' and 'lion' are masculine nouns. Similarly, 'girl', 'woman', 'queen', 'princess', 'empress', 'duchess', 'heiress', 'daughter', 'sister', 'mother', 'niece', 'wife', 'bride', 'widow', 'heroine', 'hen', 'duck', 'vixen' and 'lioness' are feminine nouns. Similarly, 'table', 'chair', 'desk', 'carpet', 'window', 'lamp', 'car', 'shop', 'dress', 'tie', 'newspaper', 'book', 'building' and 'town' are all neuter.

Some nouns in English can refer either to a man or a woman, unless the sex is indicated in the context. Such neutral nouns are sometimes said to have **dual gender**. Examples include 'author', 'singer', 'poet', 'sculptor', 'proprietor', 'teacher', 'parent', 'cousin', 'adult' and 'child'. Some words in this category were formerly automatically assumed to be masculine and several of them had feminine forms, such as 'authoress', 'poetess', 'sculptress' and 'proprietrix'. In modern times this was felt to be sexist and many of these feminine forms are now rarely used, for example, 'authoress' and 'poetess'. However some, such as actress and waitress, are still in common use. *See* -ESS.

In many languages **grammatical gender** plays a major part. In French, for example, all nouns are divided into masculine and feminine, and there is no neuter classification. Masculine nouns are preceded by *le* (definite article). Thus 'ceiling' is masculine (*le plafond*), 'hat' is masculine (*le chapeau*) and 'book' is masculine (*le livre*). Feminine nouns are preceded by *la* (definite article). Thus 'door' is feminine (*la porte*), 'dress' is feminine (*la robe*), and 'window' is feminine (*la fenêtre*).

In German there are three grammatical genders—masculine, feminine and neuter. Masculine nouns are preceded by *der* (definite article) as *der Stuhl* (the chair); feminine nouns are preceded by *die* (definite article) as *die Brücke* (the bridge); neuter nouns are preceded by *das*, as *das Brot* (bread).

Grammatical gender in English is not relevant except in the third personal singular pronouns, as 'he/him/his/himself', 'she/her/hers/herself' and 'it/it/its/itself'. Traditionally 'he', etc, was considered an acceptable pronoun not just for nouns of the masculine gender, but also for those of neutral or dual gender as well. Thus 'Every student must check that he has registered for the exam' was considered acceptable, as was 'Each passenger must be responsible for his own luggage'. Nowadays such sentences are considered sexist. In order to avoid this, some people use the 'he/she', 'his/her', etc, convention, as in 'Every employee must supply his/her own transport' and 'Each candidate must hand in his/her application form now'. People who feel this is clumsy sometimes prefer to be ungrammatical and use a plural pronoun, as in 'Every writer was told to collect their manuscripts in person' and 'Every pupil was told that they would have to be back in school by four o'clock'. It is sometimes possible to avoid being both sexist and ungrammatical by rephrasing such sentences in the plural, as in 'All pupils were told that they would have to be back in school by four o'clock'.

genitive case indicates possession or ownership. It is usually marked by *s* and an apostrophe. Many spelling errors centre on the position of the *s* in relation to the apostrophe.

Nouns in the **genitive case** are usually formed by adding *'s* to the singular noun, as in 'the girl's mother', and Peter's car'; by adding an apostrophe to plural nouns that end in *s*, as in 'all the teachers' cars' and 'the doctors' surgeries'; by adding *'s* to irregular plural nouns that do not end in *s*, as in 'women's shoes'.

In the genitive form of a name or singular noun which ends in *s*, *x* or *z*, the apostrophe may or may not be followed by *s*. In words of one syllable the final *s* is usually added, as in 'James's house', 'the fox's lair', 'Roz's dress'.

The final *s* is most frequently omitted in names, particularly in names of three or more syllables, as in 'Euripides' plays'.

In many cases the presence or absence of final *s* is a matter of convention.

Apostrophes are often omitted wrongly in modern usage, particularly in the media and by advertisers, as in 'womens hairdressers', 'childrens helpings'. In addition, apostrophes are frequently added erroneously (as in 'potato's for sale' and 'Beware of the dog's'). This is partly because people are unsure about when and when not to use them and partly because of a modern tendency to punctuate as little as possible.

A group **genitive** occurs when more than one noun is

involved, as in 'Gilbert and Sullivan's operas'. Note there is only one apostrophe *s*.

The alternative genitive construction involves the use of 'of', as in 'the mother of the girl', 'the uncle of the little girl', 'the pages of the newspaper' and 'the leg of the chair'. In general, proper nouns and animate beings tend to take the apostrophe and *s* ending and inanimate objects tend to take the 'of' construction.

geo- is a prefix derived from Greek indicating 'earth', as in 'geography', 'geology', 'geomagnetic' and 'geophysics'.

geographical features should be written with initial capital letters. These include the common nouns that are part of the name of the feature, as in 'Niagara Falls', 'Atlantic Ocean', 'River Thames', 'Mount Everest' and 'Devil's Island'.

gerund refers to the *-ing* form of a verb when it functions as a noun. It is sometimes known as a **verbal noun**. It has the same form as the present participle but has a different function. For example, in the sentence 'He was jogging down the road', 'jogging' is the present participle in the verb phrase 'was jogging', but in the sentence 'Running is his idea of relaxation', 'running' is a gerund because it acts as a noun as the subject of the sentence. Similarly, in the sentence 'We were smoking when the teacher found us', 'smoking' is the present participle in the verb phrase 'were smoking', but in the sentence 'We were told that smoking is bad for our health', 'smoking' is a gerund since it acts as a noun as the subject of the clause.

get is sometimes used to form the passive voice instead of the verb 'to be'. The use of the verb 'to **get**' to form the passive, as in 'They get married tomorrow', 'Our team got beaten today' and 'We got swindled by the con man' is sometimes considered to be more informal than the use of 'be'. Often there is more action involved when the **get** construction is used than when 'be' is used, since **get** is a more dynamic verb, as in 'She was late leaving the pub because she got involved in an argument' and in 'It was her own fault that she got arrested by the police. She hit one of the constables'.

Get is frequently overused. Such overuse should be avoided, particularly in formal contexts. **Get** can often be replaced by a synonym such as 'obtain', 'acquire', 'receive', 'get hold of', etc. Thus, 'If you are getting into money difficulties you should get some financial advice. Perhaps you could get a bank loan' could be rephrased as 'If you are in financial difficulty you should obtain some financial help. Perhaps you could receive a bank loan'.

Got, the past tense of **get**, is often used unnecessarily, as in 'She has got red hair and freckles' and 'We have got enough food to last us the week'. In these sentences 'has' and 'have' are sufficient on their own.

gliding vowel means the same as **diphthong**.

goal can be used to describe the recipient of the action of a verb, the opposite of 'agent' or 'actor'. Thus, in the sentence 'The boy hit the girl', 'boy' is the 'agent' or 'actor' and 'girl' is the **goal**. Similarly, in the sentence 'The dog bit the postman', 'dog' is the 'agent' or 'actor' and 'postman' is the **goal**.

gobbledygook is used informally to refer to pretentious and convoluted language of the type that is found in official documents and reports. It is extremely difficult to understand and should be avoided and 'plain English' used instead.

govern is used of a verb or preposition in relation to a noun or pronoun and indicates that the verb or preposition has a noun or pronoun depending on it. Thus, in the phrase 'on the table', 'on' is said to govern 'table'.

gradable is used of adjectives and adverbs and means that they can take degrees of comparison. Thus 'clean' is a **gradable** adjective since it has a comparative form (cleaner) and a superlative form (cleanest). 'Soon' is a **gradable** adverb since it has a comparative form (sooner) and a superlative form (soonest). Such words as 'supreme', which cannot normally have a comparative or superlative form, are called **non-gradable**.

-gram is a suffix derived from Greek indicating 'writing' or 'drawing', as in 'telegram', 'electrocardiogram' and 'diagram'. It is also used in modern usage to indicate a 'greeting' or 'message', as in 'kissogram'.

-graph is a suffix derived from Greek indicating 'written, recorded, represented', as in 'autograph', 'monograph', 'photograph'. It is also used to indicate 'an instrument that records', as in 'seismograph', 'tachograph' and 'cardiograph'.

group noun means the same as **collective noun**.

gynaec(o)- is a prefix derived from Greek indicating 'female, woman', as in 'gynaecology', 'gynaecium'.

H

habitual refers to the action of a verb that occurs regularly and repeatedly.. The **habitual present** is found in such sentences as 'He goes to bed at ten every night', 'She always walks to work' and 'The old man sleeps all day'. This is in contrast to the 'stative present', which indicates the action of the verb that occurs at all times, as in 'Cows chew the cud', 'Water becomes ice when it freezes', 'Children grow up' and 'We all die'. Examples of the **habitual past** tense include; 'They travelled by train to work all their lives', 'We worked twelve hours a day on that project' and 'She studied night and day for the exams'.

-hand is a suffix meaning 'worker', as in 'deckhand', 'farmhand' and 'cowhand'. It can also mean 'position', as in 'right-hand' and 'left-hand'.

haem(o)- is a prefix derived from Greek meaning 'blood', as in 'haemorrhage', 'haematology' and 'haematoma'.

haiku refers to a short Japanese poem in three unrhymed lines with an exact number of syllables per line, the syllable pattern being 5-7-5. The traditional subject matter is usually something to do with nature. A master of the form was the 17th-century Japanese poet Basho, and the following is one of his haiku:

> The | white | chrylsanlthcmum
> Even | when | liflted | to | the | eye
> Relmains | imlmacullate.

half and **halve** are liable to be confused. **Half** is a noun and **halve** is a verb. **Half** is followed by a singular noun when it is referring to an amount, as in 'Half of the milk has gone sour' and 'Half the money is hers'. It is followed by a plural verb when it is referring to a number, as in 'Half of the people are still undecided' and 'Half of the sweets are for the younger children'. The plural of **half** is **halves**, as in 'They cut the oranges in two and distributed the halves to the members of the two teams'.

The plural noun **halves** is liable to be confused with the verb **halve**. Examples of the noun **halves** include 'They served halves of grapefruit for breakfast' and 'He split the estate into halves and left it to his son and daughter'. Examples of the verb **halve** include 'halve the grapefruit for breakfast' and 'He decided to halve his estate between his son and daughter'.

hanged and **hung** are both past tense and past participles of the verb 'to hang' but they are not interchangeable. **Hung** is the more usual form, as in 'The children hung their outdoor clothes on pegs outside the classroom', 'They hung the portrait of her father in the dining room', 'Dark clouds of smoke hung over the city' and 'The boy has hung around with the same crowd of friends for years'. **Hanged** is restricted to the meaning 'suspended by the neck until dead', as in 'They hanged him for the murder of his wife in the 1920s', 'The murderer took his own life before he could be hanged', 'They had to break the news to the children that their father had hanged himself' and 'She hanged herself while the balance of her mind was disturbed'

hanging participle *see* **dangling participle**.

have is a verb which has several functions. A major use is its part in forming the 'perfect tense' and 'past perfect tense', or 'pluperfect tense', of other verb tenses. It does this in conjunction with the 'past participle' of the verb in question.

The perfect tense of a verb is formed by the present tense of the verb **have** and the past participle of the verb. Examples include 'We have acted wisely', 'They have beaten the opposition', 'The police have caught the thieves', 'The old man has died', 'The child has eaten all the food', 'The baby has fallen downstairs', 'They have grabbed all the bargains', 'You have hated him for years' and 'He has indicated that he is going to retire'. The past perfect or pluperfect is formed by the past tense of the verb **have** and the past participle of the verb in question, as in 'He had jumped over the fence', 'They had kicked in the door', 'The boy had led the other children to safety', 'His mother had made the cake', 'The headmaster had punished the pupils' and 'They had rushed into buying a new house'. Both perfect tenses and past perfect or pluperfect tenses are often contracted in speech or in informal written English, as in 'We've had enough for today', 'You've damaged the suitcase',

'You've missed the bus', 'He's lost his wallet', 'She's arrived too late', 'They'd left before the news came through', 'She'd married without telling her parents', 'He'd packed the goods himself' and 'You'd locked the door without realizing it'.

Have is often used in the phrase **have to** in the sense that something must be done. In the present tense **have to** can be used instead of 'must', as in 'You have to leave now', 'We have to clear this mess up', 'He has to get the next train' and 'The goods have to be sold today'. If the 'something that must be done' refers to the future the verb **will have to** is used', as in 'He will have to leave now to get there on time', 'The old man will have to go to hospital' and 'They'll have to move out of the house when her parents return'. If the 'something that must be done' refers to the past, **had to** is used, as in 'We had to take the injured man to hospital', 'They had to endure freezing conditions on the mountain', 'They'd to take a reduction in salary' and 'We'd to wait all day for the workman to appear'.

Have is also used in the sense of 'possess' or 'own', as in 'He has a swimming pool behind his house ', 'She has a huge wardrobe', 'We have enough food' and 'They have four cars'. In spoken or in informal English 'have got' is often used, as in 'They've got the largest house in the street', 'We've got problems now', 'They haven't got time'. This use should be avoided in formal English.

Have is also used to indicate suffering from an illness or disease, as in 'The child has measles', 'Her father has

flu' and 'She has heart disease'. **Have** can also indicate
that an activity is taking place, as in 'She's having a
shower', 'We're having a party', 'She is having a baby'
and 'They are having a dinner party'.

he is a personal pronoun and is used as the subject of a
sentence or clause to refer to a man, boy, etc. It is thus
said to be a 'masculine' personal pronoun. Since he refers to a third party and does not refer to the speaker or
the person being addressed , it is a 'third-person pronoun'. Examples include 'James is quite nice but he can
be boring', 'Bob has got a new job and he is very pleased'
and 'He is rich but his parents are very poor'.

He traditionally was used not only to refer to nouns
relating to the masculine sex but also to nouns that are
now regarded as being neutral or of 'dual gender'. Such
nouns include 'architect', 'artist', 'athlete', 'doctor',
'passenger', 'parent', 'pupil', 'singer', 'student'. Without further information from the context it is impossible
to know to which sex such nouns are referring. In modern usage it is regarded as sexist to assume such words
to be masculine by using **he** to refer to one of them unless the context indicates that the noun in question refers to a man or boy. Formerly it was considered acceptable to write or say 'Send a message to the architect who
designed the building that he is to attend the meeting'
whether or not the writer or speaker knew that the architect was a man. Similarly it was considered acceptable
to write or say 'Please tell the doctor that he is to come
straight away' whether or not the speaker or writer knew

that the doctor was in fact a man. Nowadays this convention is considered sexist. In order to avoid sexism it is possible to use the convention 'he/she', as in 'Every pupil was told that he/she was to be smartly dressed for the occasion', 'Each passenger was informed that he/she was to arrive ten minutes before the coach was due to leave' and 'Tell the doctor that he/she is required urgently'. However this convention is regarded by some people as being clumsy, particularly in spoken English or in informal written English. Some people prefer to be ungrammatical and use the plural personal pronoun 'they' instead of 'he/she' in certain situations, as in 'Every passenger was told that they had to arrive ten minutes before the coach was due to leave' and 'Every student was advised that they should apply for a college place by March'. In some cases it may be possible to rephrase sentences and avoid being either sexist or ungrammatical, as in 'All the passengers were told that they should arrive ten minutes before the coach was due to leave' and 'All students were advised that they should apply for a college place by March'.

headline is the name given to the title of a newspaper article. From the very nature of headlines they are short, partly because of shortage of space and partly to capture the attention of the would-be reader. In order to achieve this, the definite and indefinite articles and other minor words tend to be omitted, the future tense represented by a to-infinitive, as in 'Prescription charges to rise', and the present tenses used for past events. **Headline**

language, particularly that of tabloid newspapers which has to be especially succinct and eye-catching, can have an effect on the general language. Thus expressions such as 'tug-of-love', which describes the state of a child whose custody is being bitterly fought over by both parents, is now quite common in the general language but started out as a headline term. Other expressions which are typical of the language of the headlines include 'killing spree', which describes someone who loses control and kills, usually by shooting, several people indiscriminately, as in 'Local gunman goes on killing spree'. Another one is 'have-a-go', which describes an attempt by a member of the public to try and catch a criminal, as in 'Pensioner in have-a-go with bank-raider'. The language and style of **headlines** is frequently known as **headlinese**.

heading refers to a word, phrase or sentence put at the top of a page, chapter, section, etc, of a book or other printed document. These are sometimes written with initial capital letters (except for articles or prepositions), as in 'Annual Report', 'Department Budget for the Year', 'The Year Ahead', 'What Went Wrong', 'Company Plans', 'Trading Outlook Overseas', but this is a matter of taste or of house style . Some people prefer to use lower-case letters except for the first word, as in 'Sales targets for the year', 'A review of export markets', and 'The way forward'. Headings can be underlined or placed in italic type or bold type to highlight them on the page.

headword refers to a word which is at the head of an entry in a dictionary or other reference book. It is also known as 'entry word' and is usually written in bold type so that it stands out on the page and is readily identifiable.

helping verb is another name for **auxiliary verb**.

hemi- is a prefix derived from Greek meaning 'half', as in 'hemisphere' and 'hemiplegia'.

hendiadys is a figure of speech in which two nouns joined by 'and' are used to express an idea that would normally be expressed by the use of an adjective and a noun, as in 'through storm and weather' instead of 'through stormy weather'.

he/she *see* **he**.

her is a personal pronoun. It is the third person singular, is feminine in gender and acts as the object in a sentence, as in 'We saw her yesterday', 'I don't know her', 'He hardly ever sees her', 'Please give this book to her', 'Our daughter sometimes plays with her' and 'We do not want her to come to the meeting'. *See* **he**; **she**.

hers is a personal pronoun. It is the third person singular, feminine in gender and is in the poassessive case. 'The car is not hers', 'I have forgotten my book but I don't want to borrow hers', 'This is my seat and that is hers', and 'These clothes are hers'. *See* **his**; **her** and **possessive**.

hetero- is a prefix derived from Greek meaning 'other, another, different', as in 'heterodox' and 'heterosexual'.

hexa- is a prefix derived from Greek meaning 'six', as in 'hexagram' and 'hexagon'.

hiatus refers to a break in pronunciation between two

vowels that come together in different syllables, as in 'Goyaesque' and 'cooperate'.

him is the third person masculine personal pronoun when used as the object of a sentence or clause, as in 'She shot him', 'When the police caught the thief they arrested him' and 'His parents punished him after the boy stole the money'. Traditionally **him** was used to apply not only to masculine nouns, such as 'man' and 'boy', but also to nouns that are said to be 'of dual gender'. These include 'architect', 'artist', 'parent', 'passenger', 'pupil' and 'student'. Without further information from the context, it is not possible for the speaker or writer to know the sex of the person referred to by one of these words. Formerly it was acceptable to write or say 'The artist must bring an easel with him' and 'Each pupil must bring food with him'. In modern usage this convention is considered sexist and there is a modern convention that 'him/her' should be used instead to avoid sexism, as in 'The artist must bring an easel with him/her' and 'Each pupil must bring food with him/her'. This convention is felt by some people to be clumsy, particularly in spoken and in informal English, and some people prefer to be ungrammatical and use the plural personal pronoun 'them' instead, as in 'The artist must bring an easel with them' and 'Each pupil must bring food with them'. In some situations it is possible to avoid being either sexist or ungrammatical by rephrasing the sentence, as in 'All artists must bring easels with them' and 'All pupils must bring food with them. *See* **he**.

him/her *see* **him**.

his is the third personal masculine pronoun when used to
indicate possession, as in 'He has hurt his leg', 'The boy
has taken his books home' and 'Where has your father
left his tools?' Traditionally **his** was used to refer not
only to masculine nouns, such as 'man', 'boy', etc, but
to what are known as nouns 'of dual gender'. These include 'architect', 'artist', 'parent', 'passenger', 'pupil'
and 'student'. Without further information from the context it is not possible for the speaker or the writer to
know the sex of the person referred to by one of these
words. Formerly it was considered acceptable to use **his**
in such situations, as in 'Every pupil has to supply his
own sports equipment' and 'Every passenger is responsible for his own luggage'. In modern usage this is now
considered sexist and there is a modern convention that
'his/her' should be used instead to avoid sexism, as in
'Every pupil has to supply his/her own sports equipment'
and 'Every passenger is responsible for his/her own luggage'. This convention is felt by some people to be
clumsy, particularly when used in spoken or informal
written English. Some people prefer to be ungrammatical
and use the plural personal pronoun 'their', as in 'Every
pupil must supply their own sports equipment' and
'Every passenger is to be responsible for their own luggage'. In some situations it is possible to avoid being
sexist, clumsy and ungrammatical by rephrasing the sentence, as in 'All pupils must supply their own sports
equipment' and 'All passengers are to be responsible for

their own luggage.

his/her *see* **his**

holidays, in the sense of public holidays or festivals, should be written with an initial capital letter, as in 'Christmas Day', 'Easter Sunday', 'New Year' and 'Independence Day'.

holo- is a prefix meaning 'complete, whole', as in 'holistic'.

homo- is a prefix derived from Greek meaning 'same', as in 'homogenous', 'homonym', 'homograph', 'homophone' and 'homosexual'.

homograph refers to a word that is spelt the same as another word but has a different meaning and pronunciation. **Homographs** include:

bow, pronounced to rhyme with 'how', a verb meaning 'to bend the head or body as a sign of respect or in greeting, etc', as in 'The visitors bowed to the emperor' and 'The mourners bowed their heads as the coffin was lowered into the grave'.

bow, pronounced to rhyme with 'low', a noun meaning 'a looped knot, a ribbon tied in this way', as in 'She tied her hair in a bow' and 'She wears blue bows in her hair'.

lead, pronounced 'leed', a verb meaning 'to show the way', as in 'The guide will lead you down the mountain'.

lead, pronounced 'led', a noun meaning 'a type of greyish metal', as in 'They are going to remove any water pipes made from lead'.

row, pronounced to rhyme with 'low', a noun meaning

'a number of people or things arranged in a line', as in 'The princess sat in the front row'.

row, pronounced to rhyme with 'how', a noun meaning 'a quarrel, a disagreement', as in 'He has had a row with his neighbour over repairs to the garden wall'.

slough, pronounced to rhyme with 'rough', a verb meaning 'to cast off', as in 'The snake had sloughed off its old skin'.

slough, pronounced to rhyme with 'how', a noun meaning 'a swamp', as in 'Get bogged down in a slough' and 'in the Slough of Despond'.

sow, pronounced to rhyme with 'low', a verb meaning 'to scatter seeds in the earth', as in 'In the spring the gardener sowed some flower seeds in the front garden'.

sow, pronounced to rhyme with 'how', a noun meaning 'a female pig', as in 'The sow is in the pigsty with her piglets'.

homonym refers to a word that has the same spelling and the same pronunciation as another word but has a different meaning from it. Examples include:

bill, a noun meaning 'a written statement of money owed', as in 'You must pay the bill for the conversion work immediately', or 'a written or printed advertisement', as in 'We were asked to deliver handbills advertising the play'.

bill, a noun meaning 'a bird's beak', as in 'The seagull has injured its bill'.

fair, an adjective meaning 'attractive', as in 'fair young women'; 'light in colour', as in 'She has fair hair'; 'fine, not raining', as in 'I hope it keeps fair'; 'just, free from prejudice', as in 'We felt that the referee came to a fair decision'.

fair, a noun meaning 'a market held regularly in the same place, often with stalls, entertainments and rides' (now often simply applying to an event with entertainments and rides without the market), as in 'He won a coconut at the fair'; 'a trade exhibition', as in 'the Frankfurt Book Fair'.

pulse, a noun meaning 'the throbbing caused by the contractions of the heart', as in 'The patient has a weak pulse'.

pulse, a noun meaning 'the edible seeds of any of various crops of the pea family, as lentils, peas and beans', as in 'Vegetarians eat a lot of food made with pulses'.

row, a verb meaning 'to propel a boat by means of oars', as in 'He plans to row across the Atlantic single-handed'.

row, a noun meaning 'a number of people or things arranged in a line', as in 'We tried to get into the front row to watch the procession' and 'The gardener has planted rows of cabbages'.

homonym is sometimes used to describe words that are more correctly classified as **homographs** or **homophones**. *See* **homograph**; **homophone**.

homophone refers to a word that is pronounced in the same way as another but is spelt in a different way and has a different meaning. **Homophones** include:

aisle, a noun meaning 'a passage between rows of seats in a church, theatre, cinema etc', as in 'The bride walked down the aisle on her father's arm'.

isle, a noun meaning 'an island', as in 'the Isle of Wight'.

alter, a verb meaning 'to change', as in 'They have had to alter their plans'.

altar, a noun meaning 'in the Christian church, the table on which the bread and wine are consecrated for Communion and which serves as the centre of worship', as in 'The priest moved to the altar, from where he dispensed Communion', 'There is a holy painting above the altar'; or 'a raised structure on which sacrifices are made or incense burned in worship', as in 'The Druids made human sacrifices on the altar of their gods'.

ail, a verb meaning 'to be ill', as in 'The old woman is ailing'; 'to be the matter, to be wrong', as in 'What ails you?'

ale, a noun meaning 'a kind of beer', as in 'a pint of foaming ale'.

blew, a verb, the past tense of the verb 'blow', as in 'They blew the trumpets loudly'.

blue, a noun and adjective meaning 'a colour of the shade of a clear sky', as in 'She wore a blue dress'.

boar, a noun meaning 'a male pig', as in 'a dish made with wild boar'.

bore, a verb meaning 'to make tired and uninterested', as in 'The audience was obviously bored by the rather academic lecture'.

bore, a verb, the past tense of the verb 'bear', as in 'They bore their troubles lightly'.

cereal, a noun meaning 'a plant yielding grain suitable

for food', as in 'countries which grow cereal crops' and 'a prepared food made with grain', as in 'We often have cereal for breakfast'.

serial, a noun meaning 'a story or television play which is published or appears in regular parts, as in 'the final instalment of the magazine serial which she was following'.

cite, a verb meaning 'to quote or mention by way of example or proof', as in 'The lawyer cited a previous case to try and get his client off'.

sight, a noun meaning 'the act of seeing', as in 'They recognized him at first sight'.

site, a noun meaning 'a location, place', as in 'They have found a site for the new factory'.

feat, a noun meaning 'a notable act or deed', as in 'The old man received an award for his courageous feat'.

feet, a noun, the plural form of 'foot', as in 'The child got her feet wet from wading in the puddle'.

none, a pronoun meaning 'not any', as in 'They are demanding money but we have none'.

nun, a noun meaning 'a woman who joins a religious order and takes vows of poverty, chastity and obedience', as in 'She gave up the world to become a nun'.

know, a verb meaning 'to have understanding or knowledge of', as in 'He is the only one who knows the true facts of the situation', and 'to be acquainted with', as in 'I met her once but I don't really know her'.

no, an adjective meaning 'not any', as in 'We have no food left'.

rite, a noun meaning 'a ceremonial act or words,' as in 'rites involving witchcraft'.

right, an adjective meaning 'correct', as in 'Very few people gave the right answer to the question'.

write, a verb meaning 'to form readable characters', as in 'he writes regularly for the newspapers'.

stare, a verb and noun meaning 'to look fixedly' and 'a fixed gaze', as in 'She stared at him in disbelief when he told her the news' and 'He has the stare of a basilisk'.

stair, a noun meaning 'a series of flights of stairs', as in 'The old lady is too feeble to climb the stairs to her bedroom'.

-hood is a suffix meaning 'state, condition', as in 'babyhood', 'childhood', 'manhood', 'priesthood', 'womanhood' and 'widowhood'.

hydro- is a prefix derived from Greek meaning 'water, as in 'hydro-electric' and 'hydrophobia'. It also means 'hydrogen', as in 'hydrochloride'.

hyper- is a prefix derived from Greek meaning 'over, above', as in 'hyperactive', 'hypercritical', 'hyperinflation' and 'hypersensitive'.

hypo- is a prefix derived from Greek meaning 'under', as in 'hypothermia', 'hypodermic'.

hyphen refers to a small stroke used to join two words together or to indicate that a word has been broken at the end of a line because of lack of space. It is used in a variety of situations.

The **hyphen** is used as the prefixed element in a proper noun, as in 'pre-Christian', 'post-Renaissance', 'anti-

British', 'anti-Semitic', 'pro-French' and 'pro-Marxism'. It is also used before dates or numbers, as in 'pre-1914', 'pre-1066', 'post-1920', 'post-1745'. It is also used before abbreviations, as in 'pro-BBC', 'anti-EEC' and 'anti-TUC'.

The **hyphen** is used for clarification. Some words are ambiguous without the presence of a hyphen. For example, 're-cover', as in 're-cover a chair', is spelt with a hyphen to differentiate it from 'recover', as in 'The accident victim is likely to recover'. Similarly, it is used in 're-form', meaning 'to form again', as in 'They have decided to re-form the society which closed last year', to differentiate the word from 'reform', meaning 'to improve, to become better behaved', as in 'He was wild as a young man but he has reformed now'. Similarly 're-count' in the sense of 'count again', as in 're-count the number of votes cast', is spelt with a hyphen to differentiate it from 'recount' in the sense of 'tell', as in 'recount what happened on the night of the accident'.

The **hyphen** was formerly used to separate a prefix from the main element of a word if the main element begins with a vowel, as in 'pre-eminent', but there is a growing tendency in modern usage to omit the **hyphen** in such cases. At the moment both 'pre-eminent' and 'preeminent' are found. However, if the omission of the **hyphen** results in double *i*, the **hyphen** is usually retained, as in 'anti-inflationary' and 'semi-insulated'.

The **hyphen** was formerly used in words formed with the prefix *non-*, as in 'non-functional', 'non-political', 'non-flammable' and 'non-pollutant'. However there is a growing tendency to omit the hyphen in such cases, as in 'nonfunctional' and 'nonpollutant'. At the moment both forms of such words are common.

The **hyphen** is usually used with 'ex-' in the sense of 'former', as in 'ex-wife' and 'ex-president'.

The **hyphen** is usually used when 'self-' is prefixed to words, as in 'self-styled', 'a self-starter' and 'self-evident'.

Use or non-use of the **hyphen** is often a matter of choice, house style or frequency of usage, as in 'drawing-room' or 'drawing room'. and 'dining-room' or 'dining room'. There is a modern tendency to punctuate less frequently than was formerly the case and so in modern usage use of the **hyphen** in such expressions is less frequent. The length of compounds often affects the inclusion or omission of the hyphen. Compounds of two short elements that are well-established words tend not to be hyphenated, as in 'bedroom' and 'toothbrush'. Compound words with longer elements are more likely to be hyphenated, as in 'engine-driver' and 'carpet-layer'.

Some fixed compounds of two or three or more words are always hyphenated, as in 'son-in-law', 'good-for-nothing' and 'devil-may-care'

Some compounds formed from phrasal verbs are sometimes hyphenated and sometimes not. Thus both 'take-over' and 'takeover' are common, and 'run-down' and 'rundown' are both common. Again the use of the hyphen is a matter of choice. However some words formed from phrasal verbs are usually spelt without a hyphen, as in 'breakthrough'.

Compound adjectives consisting of two elements, the second of which ends in -ed, are usually hyphenated, as in 'heavy-hearted', 'fair-haired', 'fair-minded' and 'long-legged'.

Compound adjectives when they are used before nouns are usually hyphenated, as in 'gas-fired central heating', 'oil-based paints', 'solar-heated buildings' and 'chocolate-coated biscuits'.

Compounds containing some adverbs are usually hyphenated, sometimes to avoid ambiguity, as in 'his best-known opera', a 'well-known singer', 'an ill-considered venture' and 'a half-planned scheme'.

Generally adjectives and participles preceded by an adverb are not hyphenated if the adverb ends in -ly, as in 'a highly talented singer', 'neatly pressed clothes' and 'beautifully dressed young women'.

In the case of two or more compound hyphenated adjectives with the same second element qualifying the same noun, the common element need not be repeated but the **hyphen** should be, as in 'two- and three-bedroom houses' and 'long- and short-haired dogs'.

The **hyphen** is used in compound numerals from 21 to 99 when they are written in full, as in 'thirty-five gallons', 'forty-four years', 'sixty-seven miles' and 'two hundred and forty-five miles'. Compound numbers such as 'three hundred' and 'two thousand' are not hyphenated.

Hyphens are used in fractions, as in 'three-quarters', 'two-thirds', and 'seven-eighths'.

Hyphens are also used in such number phrases as 'a seventeenth-century play', 'a sixteenth-century church', 'a five-gallon pail', 'a five-year contract' and a 'third-year student'.

The other use of **hyphens** is to break words at the ends of lines. Formerly people were more careful about where they broke words. Previously, words were broken up according to etymological principles but there is a growing tendency to break words according to how they are pronounced. Some dictionaries or spelling dictionaries give help with the division and hyphenation of individual words. General points are that one-syllable words should not be divided and words should not be broken after the first letter of a word or before the last letter. Care should be taken not to break up words, for example by forming elements that are words in their own right, in such a way as to mislead the reader. Thus divisions such as 'the-rapist' and 'mans-laughter' should be avoided.

hybrid refers to a word that is formed from words or elements derived from different languages, such as 'television'.

hyperbole is a figure of speech consisting of exaggeration or over-statement, used for emphasis, as in 'I could eat a horse' and in 'I am boiling in this heat'.

I

I and **me** are liable to be confused. They are both parts of
the first person singular pronoun, but I acts as the subject of a sentence and **me** as the object. People often
assume wrongly that **me** is less 'polite' than 'I'. This is
probably because they have been taught that in answer
to such questions as 'Who is there?' the grammatically
correct reply is 'It is I'. In fact, except in formal contexts, 'It is me' is frequently found in modern usage,
especially in spoken contexts. Confusion arises as to
whether to use I or **me** after 'between'. Since 'between'
is followed by an object, **me** is the correct form. Thus it
is correct to say 'Just between you and me, I think he is
dishonest'. On the other hand, **me**, being an object,
should not be used in such sentences as 'You and I have
both been invited', 'May Jane and I play?' and 'The children and I are going to join you'. **Me** should, however,
be used in such sentences as 'The cake was made by
Mary and me', 'They were sitting in front of my son and
me at the cinema' and 'My brother and father played
against my mother and me', since in all these cases it is
the object form of the first person singular that is required.

-ian is a suffix either indicating 'a profession, job or pastime', as in 'comedian', 'musician', 'optician', 'physician', or indicating 'proper names', as in 'Elizabethan', 'Dickensian', 'Orwellian' and 'Shakesperian'.

-iana is a suffix form of -ana, indicating 'memorabilia or collections relating to people or places of note', as in 'Victoriana' and 'Churchilliana'.

-ible *see* **adjectives**.

-ics is a suffix indicating 'science' or 'study', as in 'acoustics', 'electronics', 'genetics', 'obstetrics', 'politics' and 'physics'.

ideogram refers to a written character that symbolizes a word or phrase without indicating the pronunciation, such as £, &, +.

idiolect refers to the speech habits, knowledge and command of language of an individual. This can vary considerably from person to person. For example, one person might have a much more formal **idiolect** than another.

idiom refers to an expression whose meaning cannot be easily deduced from the individual meanings of the words it contains. Thus, in the expression 'know the ropes' one can know what 'know' means and know what 'ropes' means without being able to deduce the meaning of 'know the ropes'. In fact, 'know the ropes' is a nautical idiom. If a sailor was being taught the basics of seamanship in the days of sailing ships, he would have to be taught the mechanics of ropes which were an important part of sailing in those days. Hence, 'know the ropes' has come to mean 'to understand the procedures and details involved in something', as in 'When he first started the job the trainee mechanic felt really awkward and useless, but he when he knew the ropes he felt more confident and happier'.

Similarly, one can easily understand the meanings of the various individual words in the expression 'out on a limb', but it is not at all obvious that it means idiomatically 'in a risky and often lonely position', this being a reference to someone being stuck in an isolated and precarious position on the branch of a tree. This idiom is found in sentences such as 'The young designer has gone out on a limb and produced clothes that his boss says are too experimental for the mass market'. Literally it refers to a person or animal that has crawled so far out on a branch of a tree that he/she is in danger of falling or of not being able to crawl back to the main tree.

Similarly, in the expression 'throw someone to the lions' one can easily understand the meanings of the various individual words without realizing that the expression means 'deliberately to put someone in a difficult or dangerous position', as in 'All the teachers were responsible for the change in policy with regard to school uniform but they threw the deputy head to the lions when they asked him to address a parents' meeting on the subject'. In order to appreciate the meaning of the idiom fully, the reader or listener has to understand that the idiom refers to a supposed form of entertainment in ancient Rome in which prisoners were thrown to hungry wild animals to be attacked and killed (while spectators looked on enthusiastically).

Similarly, in the expression 'throw in the towel' one can easily understand the meanings of the various individual words without realizing that the phrase means 'to give in, to admit defeat', as in 'She tried to stand up to the bullies in her school but finally she threw in the towel and asked her parents to send her to another school'. This idiom comes from the world of boxing in which 'throwing in the towel' indicates a method of conceding defeat.

Similarly, understanding the individual words of the expression 'sell someone down the river' will not help one to understand that it means 'to betray or be disloyal to someone', as in 'The bank robber who was caught by the police refused to sell his associates down the river'. The origin here is slightly more obscure in that it refers historically to slave owners in the Mississippi states of the United States, who sold their slaves to buyers downstream in Louisiana where living and working conditions were much harder.

Such idioms as 'sell someone down the river' are known as 'opaque idioms' since there is no resemblance between the meaning of the individual words of the idiom and the idiom itself. Idioms such as 'keep a straight face' are known as 'transparent idioms' since, although they are not to be interpreted literally, it is reasonably obvious what they mean.

i.e. is the abbreviation of the Latin phrase *id est* and is used before explanations or amplifications of what has just been mentioned, as in 'He was a mercenary in the war, i.e. he fought for money' and 'She is agoraphobic, i.e. she is afraid of open spaces' and 'He is a bibliophile, i.e. he loves books'. It is usually spelt with a full stop after each of the letters.

if is a conjunction which is often used to introduce a subordinate adverbial clause of condition, as in 'If he is talking of leaving he must be unhappy', 'If you tease the dog it will bite you', 'If he had realized that the weather was going to be so bad he would not have gone on the expedition', 'If I had been in charge I would have sacked him' and 'If it were a better organized firm things like that would not happen'.

If can also introduce a 'nominal' or 'noun clause', as in 'He asked if we objected' and 'She inquired if we wanted to go'.

-ify is a suffix indicating 'making or becoming', as in 'beautify', 'clarify', 'dignify', 'purify', 'satisfy' and 'simplify'.

imperative mood is the verb mood that expresses commands. The verbs in the following sentences are in the **imperative mood**. 'Go away!', 'Run faster!', 'Answer me!', 'Sit down!', 'Please get out of here!'. All of these expressions with verbs in the **imperative mood** sound rather imperious or dictatorial and usually end with an exclamation mark, but this is not true of all expressions with verbs in the **imperative mood**. For example, the following sentences all have verbs in the **imperative**

mood: 'Have another helping of ice cream', 'Help yourself to more wine', 'Just follow the yellow arrows to the X-ray department', and 'Turn right at the roundabout'. Sentences with verbs in the **imperative mood** are known as **imperative sentences**.

imperfect indicates a tense that denotes an action in progress but not complete. The term derives from the classification in Latin grammar and was traditionally applied to the 'past imperfect', as in 'They were standing there'. The **imperfect** has now been largely superseded by the 'progressive/continuous tense', which is marked by the use of 'be' plus 'present participle'. Continuous tenses are used when talking about temporary situations at a particular point in time, as in 'They were waiting for the bus'.

impersonal refers to a verb which is used with a formal subject, usually 'it', as in 'It is raining' and 'They say it will snow tomorrow'.

indefinite article: **a** and **an** are the forms of the indefinite article. The form **a** is used before words that begin with a consonant sound, as 'a box', 'a garden', 'a road', 'a wall'. The form **an** is used before words that begin with a vowel sound, as 'an apple', 'an easel', 'an ostrich', 'an uncle'. Note that it is the sound of the initial letter that matters and not the spelling. Thus **a** is used before words beginning with a *u* when they are pronounced with a *y* sound as though it were a consonant, as 'a unit', 'a usual occurrence'. Similarly, **an** is used, for example, before words beginning with the letter *h* where this is not pronounced, as in 'an heir', 'an hour', 'an honest man'.

Formerly it was quite common to use **an** before words that begin with an *h* sound and also begin with an unstressed syllable, as in 'an hotel (ho-tel)', 'an historic (his-tor-ik) occasion', 'an hereditary (her-ed-it-ary) disease'. It is now more usual nowadays to use **a** in such cases and ignore the question of the unstressed syllable.

indefinite pronouns refer to people or things without being specific as to exactly who or what they are. They include 'everyone', 'everybody', 'everything', 'anyone', 'anybody', 'anything', 'somebody', 'someone', 'something' and 'nobody', 'no one', 'nothing', as in 'Everyone is to make a contribution', 'Anyone can enter', 'Something will turn up' and 'Nobody cares'.

independent clause refers to a clause which can stand alone and make sense without being dependent on another clause, as in 'The children are safe'. Main clauses are **independent clauses**. Thus in the sentence 'She is tired and she wants to go home', there are two **independent clauses** joined by 'and'. In the sentence 'She will be able to rest when she gets home', 'She will be able to rest' is an **independent clause** and 'when she gets home' is a 'dependent clause'. In the sentence 'Because she is intelligent she thinks for herself', 'she thinks for herself' is an **independent clause** and 'because she is intelligent' is a 'dependent clause'.

indicative mood refers to the mood of a verb which denotes making a statement. The following sentences have verbs in the **indicative mood**: 'We go on holiday tomor-

row', 'He was waiting for her husband', 'They have lost
the match' and 'She will arrive this afternoon'. The **indicative mood** is sometimes known as the 'declarative
mood'. The other moods are IMPERATIVE MOOD and SUB-
JUNCTIVE MOOD.

indirect object refers to an object which can be preceded
by 'to' or 'for'. The **indirect object** usually refers to the
person who benefits from an action or receives something as the result of it. In the sentence 'Her father gave
the boy food', 'boy' is the **indirect object** and 'food' is
the 'direct object'. The sentence could be rephrased as
'Her father gave food to the boy'. In the sentence 'He
bought his mother flowers', 'his mother' is the **indirect
object** and 'flowers' is the 'direct object'. The sentence
could have been rephrased as 'he bought flowers for his
mother'. In the sentence 'They offered him a reward',
'him' is the **indirect object** and 'reward' is the 'direct
object'. The sentence could be rephrased as 'They offered a reward to him'.

indirect question refers to a question that is reported in
indirect speech, as in 'We asked them where they were
going', 'They inquired why we had come' and 'They
looked at us curiously and asked where we had come
from'.

indirect speech is also known as **reported speech** and is
a way of reporting what someone has said without using
the actual words used by the speaker. There is usually an
introductory verb and a subordinate 'that' clause, as in
'He said that he was going away', 'They announced that

they were leaving next day' and 'She declared that she had seen him there before'. In direct speech these sentences would become 'He said, "I am going away"', 'They announced, "We are leaving tomorrow"' and 'She declared, "I have seen him there before"'. When the change is made from 'direct speech' to **indirect speech**, the pronouns, adverbs of time and place and tenses are changed to accord with the viewpoint of the person doing the reporting.

infinitive refers to the 'base' form of a verb when used without any indication of person, number or tense. There are two forms of the **infinitive**. One is the 'to infinitive' form, as in 'They wished to leave', 'I plan to go tomorrow', 'We aim to please' and 'They want to emigrate', 'To know all is to forgive all', 'To err is human', 'Pull the lever to open', 'You should bring a book to read', 'The child has nothing to do', 'She is not very nice to know' and 'It is hard to believe that it happened'. The other form of the **infinitive** is called the **bare infinitive**. This form consists of the base form of the verb without 'to', as in 'We saw him fall', 'She watched him go', 'They noticed him enter', 'She heard him sigh', 'They let him go', 'I had better leave' and 'Need we return' and 'we dare not go back'. *See* SPLIT INFINITIVE.

inflect as applied to a word means to change form in order to indicate differences of tense, number, gender, case, etc. Nouns inflect for plural, as in 'ships', 'chairs', 'houses' and 'oxen'; nouns inflect for possessive, as in 'boys'', 'woman's', 'teachers'', and 'parents''; some adjectives inflect for the comparative form, as in 'brighter', 'clearer', 'shorter' and 'taller'; verbs inflect for the third person singular present tense, as in 'hears', 'joins', 'touches' and 'kicks'; verbs inflect for the present participle, as in 'hearing', 'joining', 'touching' and 'kicking'; verbs inflect for the past participle, as in 'heard', 'joined', 'touched' and 'kicked'.

inflection refers to the act of inflecting—*see* INFLECT. It also refers to an inflected form of a word or a suffix or other element used to inflect a word.

informal refers to a spoken or style of language that has a simpler grammatical structure and simpler vocabulary often involving vocabulary that is colloquial in nature or even slang.

infra- is a prefix derived from Latin indicating 'below, beneath', as in 'infrared' and 'infrastructure'.

-ing forms of verbs can be either PRESENT PARTICIPLES or GERUNDS. Present participles are used in the formation of the progressive or continuous tenses, as in 'We were looking at the pictures', 'Children were playing in the snow', 'They are waiting for the bus', 'Parents were showing their anger', 'He has been sitting there for hours'. Present participles can also be used in non-finite clauses or phrases, as in 'Walking along, she did not have a care in the world', 'Lying there, he thought about his life', 'Sighing, he left the room' and 'Smiling broadly he congratulated his friend'.

A large number of adjectives end in **-ing**. Many of these have the same form as the present participle of a transitive verb and are similar in meaning. Examples include 'an amazing spectacle', 'a boring show', 'an interesting idea', 'a tiring day', 'an exhausting climb' and 'aching limbs'. Some **-ing** adjectives are related to intransitive verbs, as 'existing problems', 'increasing responsibilities', 'dwindling resources', 'an ageing work force' and 'prevailing circumstances'. Some **-ing** adjectives are related to the forms of verbs but have different meanings from the verbs, as in 'becoming dress', 'an engaging personality', 'a dashing young man' and 'a retiring disposition'. Some **-ing** adjectives are not related to verbs at all. These include 'appetizing', 'enterprising', 'impending' and 'balding'. Some **-ing** adjectives are used informally for emphasis, as in 'a blithering idiot', 'a stinking cold' and 'a flaming cheek'.

Gerunds act as nouns and are sometimes known as 'verbal nouns'. Examples include 'Smoking is bad for one's health', 'Cycling is forbidden in the park' and 'Swimming is his favourite sport'.

intensifier refers to an adverb that affects the degree of intensity of another word. Intensifiers include 'thoroughly' in 'We were thoroughly shocked by the news', 'scarcely' in 'We scarcely recognized them' and 'totally' in 'She was totally amazed'.

inter- is a prefix of Latin origin indicating 'between', as in 'intercity', 'intercontinental' and 'interstate'.

interjections are kinds of 'exclamations'. Sometimes they are formed by actual words and sometimes they simply consist of sounds indicating emotional noises. Examples of **interjections** include 'Oh! I am quite shocked', 'Gosh! I'm surprised to hear that!', 'Phew! It's hot!', 'Ouch! That was my foot!', 'Tut-tut! He shouldn't have done that!' and 'Alas! She is dead.'

International Phonetic Alphabet is a system of written symbols designed to enable the speech sounds of any language to be consistently represented. Some of the symbols are the ordinary letters of the Roman alphabet but some have been specially invented. The alphabet was first published in 1889 and is commonly known a **IPA**.

interrogative adjective or **determiner** is an adjective or determiner that asks for information in relation to the nouns which they qualify, as in 'What dress did you choose in the end?', 'What kind of book are you looking for?', 'Which house do you like best?', 'Which pupil won the prize?', 'Whose bike was stolen?' and 'Whose dog is that?'

interrogative adverb is an adverb that asks a question, as in 'When did they leave?', 'When does the meeting start?', 'Where do they live?', 'Where was the stolen car found?', 'Where did you last see her?', 'Why was she crying?', 'Why have they been asked to leave?', 'How is the invalid?', 'How do you know that she has gone?' and 'Wherever did you find that?'

interrogative pronoun is a pronoun that asks a question, as in 'Who asked you to do that?', 'Who broke the vase?', 'What did he say?, 'What happened next?', 'Whose are those books?', 'Whose is that old car?', 'To whom was that remark addressed?' and 'To whom did you address

137

the package?'

interrogative sentence refers to a sentence that asks a question, as in 'Who is that?', 'Where is he?', 'Why have they appeared?', 'What did they take away?, 'Which do you prefer?' and 'Whose baby is that?'. Sentences which take the form of an **interrogative question** do not always seek information. Sometimes they are exclamations, as in 'Did you ever see anything so beautiful?', 'Isn't she sweet?' and 'Aren't they lovely?'. Sentences which take the form of questions may really be commands or directives, as in 'Could you turn down that radio?', 'Would you make less noise?' and 'Could you get her a chair?'. Sentences which take the form of questions may function as statements, as in 'Isn't there always a reason?' and 'Haven't we all experienced disappointment?'. Some **interrogative sentences** are what are known as 'rhetorical questions', which are asked purely for effect and require no answer, as in 'Do you think I am a fool?', 'What is the point of life?' and 'What is the world coming to?'.

intra- is a prefix of Latin origin indicating 'within', as 'intramuscular', 'intra-uterine' and 'intravenous'.

intransitive verb refers to a verb that does not take a 'direct object', as in 'Snow fell yesterday', 'The children played in the sand', 'The path climbed steeply', 'Time will tell', 'The situation worsened', 'Things improved' and 'Prices increased'. Many verbs can be either transitive or intransitive, according to the context. Thus 'play' is **intransitive** in the sentence 'The children played in the sand' but 'transitive' in the sentence 'The boy plays the piano'. Similarly 'climb' is intransitive in the sentence 'The path climbs steeply' but transitive in the sentence 'The mountaineers climbed Everest'. Similarly 'tell' is **intransitive** in the sentence 'Time will tell' but 'transitive' in the sentence 'He will tell his life story'.

introductory it refers to the use of 'it' as the subject of a sentence in the absence of a meaningful subject. It is used particularly in sentences about time and the weather, as in 'It is midnight', 'It is dawn', 'It is five o'clock', 'It is twelve noon', 'It is raining', 'It was snowing', 'It was windy' and 'It was blowing a gale'.

intrusive r refers to the pronunciation of the *r* sound between two words or syllables where the first of these ends in a vowel sound and the second begins with a vowel sound and where there is no 'r' in the spelling. It appears in such phrases as 'law and order', which is frequently pronounced as 'lawr and order'.

invariable refers to a word whose form does not vary by inflection. Such words include 'sheep' and 'but'.

inversion refers to the reversal of the usual word order. It particularly refers to subjects and verbs. **Inversion** is used in questions, in some negative sentences, and for literary effect. In questions, an auxiliary verb is usually put in front of the subject and the rest of the verb group is put after the subject, as in 'Are you going to see her?' and 'Have they inspected the goods yet?'. The verb 'to do' is frequently used in **inversion**, as in 'Did he commit the crime?' and 'Do they still believe that?'. Examples of the use of **inversion** in negative sentences include 'Seldom have I witnessed such an act of selfishness', 'Never had she experienced such pain' and 'Rarely do we have time to admire the beauty of the countryside'. This use in negative sentences is rather formal.

Inversion frequently involves adverbial phrases of place, as in 'Beyond the town stretched field after field', 'Above them soared the eagle' and 'Along the driveway grew multitudes of daffodils'.

Inversion is also found in conditional clauses that are not introduced by conjunction, as in 'Had you arrived earlier you would have got a meal' and 'Had we some more money we could do more for the refugees'.

inverted commas, also called **quotation marks** and **quotes**, are used to enclose material that is part of reported speech. *See* REPORTED SPEECH. They can also be used instead of italic type in the titles of books, newspapers, magazines, plays, films, musical works, works of art, etc, as in 'The Times', 'Northanger Abbey' by Jane Austen, 'Two Gentlemen of Verona', 'The Silence of the Lambs' and 'The Mikado'. **Inverted commas** can also be used to emphasize or draw attention to a particular word or phrase, as in 'She wants to know how to spell "picnicked"'. **Inverted** commas can either be single or double. If a word, phrase or passage is already contained within quotes one should use the opposite style of **inverted commas** to the set already in use, as in 'She asked how to pronounce "controversy"' or "She asked how to pronounce 'controversy'".

irony indicates the use of a word or words to convey something that is completely different from the literal meaning, as in 'I don't suppose you'd be interested to hear that your house has been burgled', 'So you've crashed the car. Thanks! That's a great help!'. *See* DRAMATIC IRONY.

irregular plurals refer to the plural form of nouns that do not form their plural in the regular way. Most nouns in English add -*s* to the singular form to form the plural form, as in 'boy' to 'boys'. Some add -*es* to the singular form to form the plural, as in 'church' to 'churches'. Nouns ending in a consonant followed by -*y* have -*ies* as a regular plural ending. Thus 'fairy' becomes 'fairies' and 'berry' becomes 'berries'. The foregoing are all examples of 'regular plurals'.

Irregular plurals include words that are different in form from the singular forms and do not simply add an ending. These include 'men' from 'man', 'women' from 'woman' and 'mice' from 'mouse'. Some irregular plurals are formed by changing the vowel of the singular forms, as in 'feet' from 'foot', 'geese' from 'goose' and 'teeth' from 'tooth'. Some irregular plural forms are formed by adding -*en*, as 'oxen' from 'ox' and 'children' from 'child'. Some nouns ending in -*f* form plurals in -*ves*, as in 'loaf' to 'loaves', 'half' to 'halves', 'wife' to 'wives' and 'wolf' to 'wolves', but some have alternative endings, as 'hoof' to either 'hoofs' or 'hooves', and some form regular plurals unchanged, as 'roof' to 'roofs'. Some irregular plural forms are the original foreign plural forms of words adopted into English, for example 'stimuli' from 'stimulus', 'phenomena' from 'phenomenon', 'criteria' from 'criterion', 'larvae' from 'larva'. In modern usage there is a growing tendency to anglicize the plural forms of foreign words. Many of these co-exist with the plural form, for example 'thesauruses' and 'thesauri', 'formulas' and 'formulae', 'gateaus' and 'gateaux' and 'indexes' and 'indices'. Sometimes the anglicized plural formed according to the regular English rules differs slightly in meaning from the irregular foreign plural. Thus 'indexes' usually applies to guides in books and 'indices' is usually used in mathematics. Some nouns have irregular plurals in that the plural form the singular form are the same. These include 'sheep', 'grouse' (the game-bird) and 'salmon'. Some nouns have a regular plural and an irregular plural form .Thus 'brother' has the plural forms 'brothers' and 'brethren' although 'brethren' is now mainly used in a religious context and is archaic in general English.

irregular adjectives refer to adjectives that do not conform to the usual rules of forming the comparison and superlative. Many adjectives either add -*er* for the comparative and add -*est* for the superlative, as in 'taller', 'shorter' and 'tallest', 'shortest'. Some adjectives form their comparatives with 'more' and their superlatives with 'most', as in 'more beautiful', 'more practical' and 'most beautiful', 'most practical'. **Irregular adjectives** do not form their comparatives and superlatives in either of these ways. Irregular adjectives include:

positive	comparative	superlative
good	better	best
bad	worse	worst
little	less	least
many	more	most

irregular verbs are verbs that do not conform to the usual pattern of verbs in that some of their forms deviate from what one would expect if the pattern of regular verbs was being followed. There are four main forms of a regular verb—the INFINITIVE or 'base' form, as in 'hint', 'halt', 'hate' and 'haul'; the 'third-person singular' form as 'hints', 'halts', 'hates' and 'hauls'; the -ING form or 'present participle', as 'hinting', halting', 'hating' and 'hauling'; the -*ed* form or 'past tense' or 'past participle', as 'hinted', halted', 'hated' and 'hauled.

Irregular verbs deviate in some way from that pattern, in particular from the pattern of adding -*ed* to the past tense and past participle. They fall into several categories.

One category concerns those which have the same form in the past tense and past participle forms as the infinitive and do not end in -*ed*, like regular verbs. These include:

infinitive	past tense	past participle
bet	bet	bet
burst	burst	burst
cast	cast	cast
cost	cost	cost
cut	cut	cut

hit	hit	hit
hurt	hurt	hurt
let	let	let
put	put	put
run	run	run
set	set	set
shed	shed	shed
shut	shut	shut
slit	slit	slit
split	split	split
spread	spread	spread

Some **irregular verbs** have two past tenses and two past participles which are the same, as in:

infinitive	*past tense*	*past participle*
burn	burned, burnt	burned, burnt,
dream	dreamed, dreamt	dreamed, dreamt,
dwell	dwelled, dwelt	dwelled, dwelt,
hang	hanged, hung,	hanged, hung
kneel	kneeled, knelt,	kneeled, knelt
lean	leaned, leant	learned, learnt
leap	leaped, leapt,	leaped, leapt
learn	learned, learnt	learned, learnt
light	lighted, lit	lighted, lit
smell	smelled, smelt	smelled, smelt
speed	speeded, sped	speeded, sped
spill	spilled, spilt	spilled, spilt
spoil	spoiled, spoilt	spoiled, spoilt
weave	weaved, woven	weaved, woven
wet	wetted, wet	wetted, wet,

Some **irregular verbs** have past tenses which do not end in *-ed* and have the same form as the past participle. These include:

infinitive	*past tense*	*past participle*
become	became	became
bend	bent	bent
bleed	bled	bled
breed	bred	bred
build	built	built
cling	clung	clung
come	came	came
dig	dug	dug
feel	felt	felt
fight	fought	fought
find	found	found
flee	fled	fled
fling	flung	flung
get	got	got
grind	ground	ground
hear	heard	heard
hold	held	held
keep	kept	kept
lay	laid	laid
lead	led	led
leave	left	left
lend	lent	lent
lose	lost	lost
make	made	made
mean	meant	meant

irregular verbs

meet	met	met
pay	paid	paid
rend	rent	rent
say	said	said
seek	sought	sought
sell	sold	sold
send	sent	sent
shine	shone	shone
shoe	shod	shod
sit	sat	sat
sleep	slept	slept
slide	slid	slid
sling	slung	slung
slink	slunk	slunk
spend	spent	spent
spin	spun	spun
stand	stood	stood
stick	stuck	stuck
sting	stung	stung
strike	struck	struck
string	strung	strung
sweep	swept	swept
swing	swung	swung
teach	taught	taught
tell	told	told
think	thought	thought
understand	understood	understood
weep	wept	wept
win	won	won

| wring | wrung | wrung |

Some **irregular verbs** have regular past tense forms but two possible past participles, one of which is regular. These include:

infinitive	past tense	past participle
mow	mowed	mowed, mown
prove	proved	proved, proven
sew	sewed	sewn, sewed
show	showed	showed, shown
sow	sowed	sowed, sown
swell	swelled	swelled, swollen

Some **irregular verbs** have past tenses and past participles that are different from each other and different from the infinitive. These include:

infinitive	past tense	past participle
arise	arose	arisen
awake	awoke	awoken
bear	bore	borne
begin	began	begun
bid	bade	bidden
bite	bit	bitten
blow	blew	blown
break	broke	broken
choose	chose	chosen
do	did	done
draw	drew	drawn
drink	drank	drunk
drive	drove	driven
eat	ate	eaten

irregular verbs

fall	fell	fallen
fly	flew	flown
forbear	forbore	forborne
forbid	forbade	forbidden
forgive	forgave	forgiven
forget	forgot	forgotten
forsake	forsook	forsaken
freeze	froze	frozen
forswear	forswore	forewarn
give	gave	given
go	went	gone
grow	grew	grown
hew	hewed	hewn
hide	hid	hidden
know	knew	known
lie	lay	lain
ride	rode	ridden
ring	rang	rung
saw	sawed	sawn
see	saw	seen
rise	rose	risen
shake	shook	shaken
shrink	shrank	shrunk
slay	slew	slain
speak	spoke	spoken
spring	sprang	sprung
steal	stole	stolen
stink	stank	stunk
strew	strewed	strewn

148

stride	strode	stridden
strive	strove	striven
swear	swore	sworn
swim	swam	swum
take	took	taken
tear	tore	torn
throw	threw	thrown
tread	trod	trodden
wake	woken	woke
wear	wore	worn
write	written	wrote

-ise and **-ize** are both verb endings. In British English there are many verbs which can be spelt ending in either **-ise** or **-ize**, as 'computerise/ize', 'economise/ize', 'finalist/ize', 'hospitalise/ize', 'modernise/ize', 'organise/ize', 'realise/ize', 'theorise/ize'. There are a few verbs which cannot be spelt **-ize**. These include 'advertise', 'advise', 'comprise', 'despise', 'exercise', 'revise', 'supervise' and 'televise'.

-ish is a suffix indicating 'somewhat', as in 'baldish', 'biggish', 'smallish', 'youngish', and 'nationality', as 'Spanish', 'Turkish' and 'Polish'.

-ism is a suffix indicating 'state, condition', as in 'alcoholism', 'fatalism', 'heroism' and 'plagiarism', or indicating 'doctrine, movement, system, theory', as in 'Catholicism', 'Marxism' and 'Thatcherism'. It now also indicates 'discrimination', as in 'ageism', 'sexism', 'racism'.

iso- is a prefix indicating 'equal', as in 'isobar', 'isotherm' and 'isosceles'.

-ist is a suffix indicating 'believer, supporter, practitioner', as in 'atheist', 'fascist', 'feminist' and 'Methodist'.

italic type refers to a sloping typeface that is used for a variety of purposes. It is used to differentiate a piece of text from the main text, which is usually in Roman type. For example, it is used sometimes for the titles of books, newspapers, magazines, plays, films, musical works and works of art, as in 'he is a regular reader of *The Times*', 'She reads *Private Eye*', 'Have you read *Animal Farm* by George Orwell', 'He has never seen a production of Shakespeare's *Othello*', 'We went to hear Handel's *Messiah*', '*Mona Lisa* is a famous painting'. Sometimes such titles are put in quotation marks rather than in italic.

Italic type is also sometimes used for the names of ships, trains, etc, as in 'the launch of *The Queen Elizabeth II*', 'She once sailed in *The Queen Mary*' and 'Their train was called *The Flying Scotsman*'.

Italic type is also used for the Latin names of plants and animals, as in 'of the genus *Lilium*', 'trees of the genus *Pyrus*, *Panthera pardus* and *Canis lupus*.

Italic type is sometimes used for foreign words that have been adopted into the English language but have never been fully integrated. Examples include *bête noire*, *raison d'être*, *inter alia* and *Weltschmerz*.

Italic type can also sometimes be used to draw attention to a particular word, phrase or passage, as in 'How do you pronounce *formidable*?', or to emphasize a word or phrase, as in 'Is he *still* in the same job?'

-ite is a suffix which can indicate 'believer, supporter, practitioner', as in 'Thatcherite' and 'Trotskyite'.

-itis is a suffix indicating 'illness or disease', as in 'bronchitis', 'hepatitis' and 'meningitis'.

its and **it's** are liable to be confused. **Its** is an adjective meaning 'belonging to it', as in 'The house has lost its charm' and 'The dog does not like its kennel'. **It's** means 'it is', as in 'Do you know if it's raining?' and 'It's not fair to expect her to do all the chores'.

-ize *see* **-ise**.

J

jargon refers to the technical or specialist language used among members of a particular profession or area. It is often used as a derogatory term to describe unnecessarily obscure or pretentious language used within a profession and incomprehensible to members of the public who might come into contact with it and require to know what is being talked about. **Jargon** should be avoided in any document or situation involving lay people who have no specialist knowledge of the subject being referred to or of the language associated with it. **Jargon** in some professions easily becomes **goddledegook**.

journalese is a derogatory name for the style of writing and choice of vocabulary supposedly found in newspapers. It is usually the style of writing in tabloid newspapers, such as widespread use of clichés, sensational language and short sentences, that is meant by the term. *See* HEADLINE.

jussive refers to a type of clause or sentence that expresses a command, as in 'Do be quiet! I'm trying to study', 'Let's not bother going to the party. I'm too tired', 'Would you pass me that book' and 'Look at that everybody! The river has broken its banks'.

just is an adverb which indicates that something happened a short time previously. In British English it is usually used with the perfect tense of the verb which it accompanies, as in 'I have just finished work', 'We have just decided to buy a new car', 'You've just missed the bus' and 'She's just passed her driving test'.

In American English **just** usually accompanies the past tense of the verb, and some speakers of British English do also, especially in an informal context, as in 'I just saw a bad accident on the motorway', 'We just noticed that it's snowing' and 'He just left'.

Just has more than meaning. It can also mean 'only' and 'exactly'. In the sense of 'only', care should be taken to position it in the correct place in the sentence. For example, in the sentence 'He drank just two glasses of wine', it means that he drank only two glasses of wine, but in the sentence 'He just drank two glasses of wine' it means that he very recently drank two glasses of wine. To add to the confusion, although people may be careful about the positioning of **just** in formal writing they tend not to be in informal writing or speech. Thus someone could say in reply to the questions 'How much has he had to drink? Is he fit to drive?', 'He just had two glasses of wine', meaning that that was all he had drunk. In speech the meaning is usually obvious from intonation and context.

Just can also be used in the sense of 'only' in such sentences as 'Just Peter went on holiday with his parents. The other children stayed at home' and 'Just one

coat was left on the stall. The rest were sold early on'.
Again care should be taken to place *just* before the word
it refers to in order to avoid ambiguity.

Just can also mean 'exactly', as in 'I see you have a
food processor. That's just what I need' and 'Where did
you find that cape? That's just what I've been looking
for'.

K

kibbutzim is an example of an irregular plural form. Most nouns in English form plurals by adding *-s* or *-es* to the singular form, as in 'book and books' and 'church and churches'. However several words of foreign origin which have been adopted into English but not fully integrated retain the plural form found in the foreign language. **Kibbutz**, meaning a communal settlement in Israel, is one such word. Of Hebrew origin, it retains the plural form **kibbutzim**. In some cases there is a growing tendency for foreign plurals to be anglicized, or to exist alongside an anglicized plural, as in 'thesauruses/thesauri', but this is not yet the case with **kibbutzim**.

kilo- is a prefix indicating 'a thousand', as in 'kilogram', 'kilohertz', 'kilolitre', 'kilometre' and 'kilowatt'.

-kin is a suffix which indicates 'a diminutive or smaller version', as in 'lambkin' and 'mannikin'.

kind as a noun can cause grammatical problems. It is used to refer to a class of people or things. Since it is a 'count' noun, it should take the plural form 'kinds' after words such as 'all' and 'many', as in 'He met all kinds of people when he was travelling round the world', 'We found all kinds of treasure when we were clearing out the attic' and 'We found all kinds of wild flower in the meadows'. A singular noun should follow 'kinds of', as in 'We found all kinds of treasure' but it is quite common for people to use a plural noun instead, as in 'We found all kinds of treasures'. This is best restricted to informal or spoken use.

'These' and 'those' are frequently found preceding **kind of,** as in 'She doesn't like these kind of cakes' and 'My mother used to make those kind of biscuits' but this is incorrect and 'this' and 'that' should be used, as in 'I don't like that kind of joke' and 'My mother prefers this kind of holiday'.

The use of 'kind of' to mean 'somewhat' or 'rather', as in 'I'm kind of hungry', 'She's kind of rude to him' and It's kind of cold in there' should be restricted to informal speech or dialect. This phrase is sometimes written 'kinda', as in 'We're kinda bored'.

Kind is also used as an adjective meaning 'caring' or 'generous', as in 'A kind old lady lent the children money to get a bus home', 'It was kind of you to let them borrow your car' and 'Children should be taught to be kind to animals'.

-kind is a suffix indicating 'a group of people', as in 'humankind', 'mankind', 'womankind'.

kindly looks like an adverb but it can be either an adverb or an adjective. As an adverb it means 'in a kind or caring manner' or 'generously', as in 'They treated us kindly during our stay', 'Her parents kindly treated us to a meal in a restaurant' and 'They very kindly offered us a lift'.

The adverb **kindly** is also used in rather an ironic way when the user is annoyed, as in 'Would you kindly stop allowing your dog to foul the pavement'. It is also used in the phrase 'not to take kindly to', meaning 'to be unwilling to accept', as in 'The new pupil doesn't take kindly to discipline', 'He won't take kindly to being kept waiting' and 'The candidate was so confident that he is unlikely to take kindly to being rejected'.

Kindly is more common as an adjective and means 'kind, warm, friendly', as in 'a kindly old lady who was always helping her neighbours' and 'She gave the children a kindly smile'.

kneel is one of several verbs in English which have more than one past participle and past tense form. The past participle and past tense can both be either 'kneeled' or 'knelt', as in 'The child knelt in prayer', 'She kneeled before the altar' and 'She had knelt at her dying husband's bedside every night' and 'They had kneeled in supplication before the emperor but he spurned them'. Although both 'knelt' and 'kneeled' are acceptable forms in British English, 'knelt' is the more common form.

L

laid and **lain** are liable to be confused. **Laid** is the past
tense and past participle of the verb 'lay', meaning 'to
place or put', as in 'She laid the antique vase carefully
on the table', 'He laid the new carpet tiles in the hall',
'They have laid the baby on a mat on the floor' and 'We
have laid vinyl tiles on the kitchen floor'. **Lain** is the
past participle of the verb 'lie', 'to rest in a horizontal
position', as in 'Those letters have lain on his desk all
week', 'The dead man had lain in the empty house for
several days', and 'They had lain on the beach in the
midday sun'.

language refers to the means by which human beings communicate using words, as in 'Children acquire language
at different rates. Some speak much earlier than others'.
Language can refer either to spoken or written communication. It can also refer to the variety of communication used by a particular nation or state, as in 'He visits
France regularly but makes no attempt to understand the
French language', 'He won't start to learn a foreign language until he goes to secondary school' and 'People in
other parts of Europe tend to speak more languages than
the British'. The language that a person speaks from birth

is known as his/her 'first language' or 'mother tongue'. He/she is said to be a native speaker of this language.

Language can also be used to refer to the style and vocabulary of a piece of writing, as in 'The language of his novels is very poetic'.

Language can also apply to the particular style and variety of language that is used in a particular profession or among a particular group of people with some common interest, as in 'legal language', 'scientific language', 'technical language', etc. Such technical or specialist language is sometimes referred to rather pejoratively as 'jargon' or as 'legalese', 'medicalese', 'computerese', etc.

A person's own style of **language** with regard to vocabulary, structure, etc, is known as 'ideolect', as in 'He is the son of academic parents and has rather a formal ideolect'.

The **language** of a region or community with regard to vocabulary, structure, grammar and pronunciation is known as 'dialect', as in 'the dialect of the North-East of England'.

last can be an adverb or an adjective. As an adjective it can give rise to ambiguity. It can mean 'coming after all others, final', as in 'He was the last runner to hit the finishing tape', 'That was the last novel he wrote before he died', 'He did not die until he was 90 but he wrote his last novel at the age of 40'. Ambiguity arises when **last** takes on other meanings. For example, it is frequently used as a synonym for 'latest', as in 'I really enjoyed his last novel and I'm looking forward to the next'. In this particular sentence it is clear that **last** means 'latest' not 'final' but this is not always the case. For example, in the sentence 'He was 60 when he directed his last film', it is not at all clear from the evidence of the sentence alone whether it is his 'final' or 'latest' film that is being referred to. Thus it is better to use either 'final' or 'latest' rather than 'last' in order to clarify the meaning.

Confusion can arise also between **last** meaning 'final' and **last** meaning 'preceding', as in 'I did not quite understand the last chapter'. On the evidence of the sentence alone, it is not clear whether **last** refers to the preceding chapter or to the final chapter. Again it is best to avoid ambiguity by using a synonym for **last**.

Yet more confusion can be caused with regard to **last** when it is used to refer to days of the week. It varies from person to person whether 'last Saturday' refers to the Saturday that has just gone or to the one before that. To some extent it depends which day of the week it is when the statement is made. To avoid ambiguity it is best to specify the date.

Last is also used as an adverb, as in 'They last saw their father when he was going to war', 'When the family go to the dentist my brother always wants to go in last' and 'If you are adding cream to the soup you add it last'. The adverbial use does not suffer from problems of ambiguity.

latest is an adjective that is liable to be confused with **last**-*see* LAST. It can also mean 'most up-to-date', 'most fashionable', as in 'the very latest dresses from the Paris designers'. **Latest** is also found in this meaning in the phrase 'the very latest', as in 'she always dresses in the very latest'. It can also mean 'most late', the superlative of 'late' in the sense of 'far on in the day or night', as in 'The latest train which you can get from that station leaves at ten o' clock'. In this sense **latest** is also found in the phrase 'at the latest' and in the phrase 'at the very latest', meaning 'most late time', as in 'You must arrive at the station at ten o'clock at the latest' and 'The students' essays must be handed in by Friday at the very latest'.

lay and **lie** are liable to be confused. This is because **lay** as well as being a verb in its own right is also one of the principal parts of **lie**—the past tense as in 'They lay on the beach in the sun', 'The books lay on the table gathering dust' and 'She lay on her bed and wept'.

Lay is a transitive verb meaning 'to place or put', as in 'She asked him to lay new tiles in the kitchen' and 'She had to lay down her shopping to open the door'. The principal parts of **lay** are 'lays' (third person singular present), as in 'She always lays the baby on the grass to play'; 'laying' (present participle), as in 'Laying her shopping down she put her key in the lock'; 'laid' (past participle and past tense), as in 'She laid the package on the table' and 'He had laid his car keys on the table and forgotten about them'.

Lie is an intransitive verb whose principlal parts are 'lies' (third person singular present), as in 'Their house lies to the north of the village'; 'lying' (present participle), as in 'Lying on the grass they looked up at the sky'; 'lay' (past tense), as in 'The climbers lay on the summit exhausted'; 'lain' (past participle), as in 'Those books have lain there for weeks'.

Lie has another totally unrelated meaning. It means 'to say or write something that is untrue', as in 'You didn't have to lie about your part in the affair'. The principal parts of the verb **lie** are 'lies' (third person singular present), as in 'lies about why he arrives home late from work'; 'lying' (present participle), as in 'Lying, he looked her straight in the face'; 'lied' (past participle and past tense), as in 'He lied to his employers about his qualifications' and 'she suddenly realized that he had lied all the time'.

lean is one of several verbs in English which have two forms of the past tense and the past participle, 'leaned' and 'leant', as in 'She leaned over the fence to talk to her neighbour', 'He leaned over his desk to catch the attention of his colleagues', 'They have leaned over backwards to help her' and 'She has leant down to pick something up and hurt her back'. The two forms are interchangeable.

leap is one of several verbs in English which have two forms of the past tense and past participle, 'leaped' and 'leapt', as in 'The children leaped around the park in high spirits', 'She leapt up in surprise when she heard the news', 'She had leaped over a high fence and broken her leg' and 'The child has leapt over the steam and run off'. The two forms are virtually interchangeable but 'leapt' is more common in British English.

learn is one of several verbs in English which have two forms of the past tense and past participle, 'learned' and 'learnt', as in 'They learned French at school', 'She learnt to ski in Austria', 'I think the boys have learned their lesson' and 'He had learnt to be grateful for what he was given'. The forms are interchangeable. 'Learned' as a past tense or past participle should not be confused with 'learned', the adjective meaning 'erudite, well-read, intellectual', as in 'Students filled the lecture hall to listen to the learned professor' and 'The company publishes learned journals'. This adjective is pronounced with two syllables—*ler-nid*—whereas 'learned', the past tense and past participle, is pronounced as one syllable—*lernd*.

length mark is a mark used in phonetics in relation to a vowel to indicate that it is long. This can take the form of a 'macron', a small horizontal stroke placed above a letter, or a symbol resembling a colon placed after a vowel in the IPA pronunciation system.

-less is a suffix meaning 'without, lacking' added to nouns to form adjectives, as in 'characterless', 'clueless', 'expressionless', 'fearless', 'flawless', 'harmless', 'homeless', 'hopeless', 'passionless', 'toothless' and 'useless'. It can also mean 'without being able to be measured', as in 'ageless', 'countless', 'priceless' and 'timeless'.

less and **fewer** are liable to be confused. *See* FEWER.

-let is a suffix indicating a diminutive or smaller form of something, as in 'booklet', 'coverlet', 'droplet', 'islet', 'piglet', 'starlet' and 'streamlet'.

letter-writing has become something of a dying art in view
of the widespread use of the telephone. However, all of
us from time to time have to write some form of letter
and many of these are business letters. There are a few
conventions in formal letters that should be observed.

One's own address, including one's postcode, should
be placed at the right-hand side of the page. Each line of
one's own address should be indented slightly below the
one above and the date put below the last line of the
address, as in:

> 23 Park Drive
> Raleigh
> Blackshire
> RA14 2TY
>
> 5 June 1993

Whether one puts a comma at the end of the various
lines of the address is a matter of taste. It is becoming
common in modern usage not to do so.

One's telephone number can either be placed between
the postcode and the date or at the other side of the page
on the same line as the first line of the address.

If one is writing a business letter one should also put
the address of the person to whom one is writing. It
should be placed at the other side of the page below one's
own address and the lines of this should be placed di-
rectly below each other without being indented, as in:

23, Park Drive
Raleigh
Blackshire
RA 14 2TY.

5 June 1993.

The Manager Eastlands Bank
33 West Street
Northlands
Blackshire
NR15 3RJ.

With regard to deciding how to address the person to whom one is writing it is best to find out his/her name. Having done so then one can start the letter off, as in :

Dear Mr White,

If one is writing to a woman the situation is slightly more problematic. Formerly it was considered acceptable to address the person written to as 'Miss' if one knew her to be unmarried or as 'Mrs' if one knew her to be married. If one did not know her marital status one could either use 'Miss' or use the 'Madam' convention. In modern usage 'Ms' is the acceptable term if one does not know the marital status of the woman to whom one is writing. Many people prefer to use this designation even if they do know the person's marital status and many women prefer to be addressed in this way. On the other hand, some women, especially older women, do not like the 'Ms' designation.

In modern usage some people prefer to put the first name and surname of the relevant person instead of the surname preceded by Mr, etc, as in:

Dear John White,

The above style of address is considered rather informal by some people.

If it is not easy to ascertain the name of the person to whom one wishes to write then it is perfectly acceptable to address him/her in terms of their position or job, as in:

Dear manager,

Dear Personnel Manager,

Dear Area Manager,

In formal letters it is also acceptable to use 'Sir' or 'Madam', as in:

Dear Sir,

Dear Madam,

Dear Sir/Madam,

Obviously the above style of address is used in cases where one does not know the sex of the person to whom one is writing.

In ending a formal letter it was traditionally the custom to write 'Yours faithfully' before one's signature, if one had addressed the person written to as 'Dear sir' or 'Dear madam', as in :

> Yours faithfully,
> Jane Black.

It was also the custom to end the letter with 'Yours sincerely' if the letter was either informal in nature or a formal letter which began with 'Dear Mr White' etc, as in:

> Yours sincerely,
> Mary Brown.

In modern usage it is now considered acceptable to end a letter with 'Yours sincerely' even if one has begun it with 'Dear sir', etc. 'Yours faithfully' is considered exceptionally formal.

It is common to end even business letters with 'Kind regards', especially if the person written to is known to one.

On the envelope the lines can be indented or not, according to taste. Each line, except the last one, can have a comma after or not. However, in modern usage there is an increasing tendency to punctuate as little as possible and the commas are frequently omitted, as in:

Ms Mary Brown
29 Lower Forth Street
Redwood
Blackshire
RD16 5YP.

The same comments on Mrs, Miss and Ms apply to envelopes as apply to the opening greeting in letters. *See above*. Anything that can be done to make the address as clear as possible should be done. It is important always to put the postcode as failure to do so slows down delivery of the letter. It is also advisable to highlight the town one is sending the letter to, either by putting it in capital letters, or by underlining it, as in:

Mr James Green
45, Park Avenue
BOSTON
Blackshire
BT16 6GH.

In modern usage it is becoming increasingly common to write the full name of the person written to on the envelope, as in:

James Black
36, High Street
BLANKTON
Blankshire
BL13 9T2.

It is considered formal or old-fashioned to use 'Esq.', usually spelt with a full stop at the end and preceded by a comma. If used, 'Esq.' should be placed after the mans's name and there should be no accopmanying 'Mr', as in:

John Brown, Esq
43 Queen Street
Whiteoaks
Blankshire
WH12 TY.

lexicography refers to the art and practice of defining words, selecting them and arranging them in dictionaries and glossaries.

licence and **license** are liable to be confused. **Licence** is a noun referring to 'a document indicating that official permission or authorization has been given to do something', as in 'He does not have a current driving licence', 'You need a trading licence to sell goods there' and 'The pub owner lost his licence'. **Licence** also means 'too great freedom, disregard for rules of behaviour, social acceptability, morals, etc', as in 'The organizers of the concert objected to the licence shown by the young people in their dress'. In this sense the word **licence** is usually used in formal situations.

License is a verb meaning 'to give a licence to, to give official permission or authorization to', as in 'He is licensed to sell alcohol', 'She is not licensed to sell goods in the market' and 'The restaurant is not licensed but you can bring your own wine'. **Licence** is often misspelt as **license**.

The above comments refer to British English. In American English **license** is used for both the noun and the verb.

lie *see* **lay**.

ligature

ligature refers to a printed character combining two letters in one, as in æ and œ. It is sometimes called a 'digraph'.

-like is a suffix indicating similarity, as in 'childlike',
'cowlike', 'dreamlike', 'ladylike', 'lifelike' and 'warlike'.

-ling is a suffix indicating a diminutive or smaller version
of something, as in 'duckling', 'gosling' and 'nestling'.

-logue is a suffix derived from Greek meaning 'indicating
'conversation, discussion', as in 'dialogue', 'epilogue',
'monologue', 'prologue' and 'travelogue'.

limerick refers to a humorous five-lined piece of light
verse, with the first two lines rhyming with each other,
the third and fourth lines rhyming with each other, and
the fifth line rhyming with the first line. Usually there
are three stressed beats in the first, second and fifth lines
and two stressed beats on the third and fourth lines. Traditionally the name of a place is mentioned in the first
line and may be repeated in the last line. Edward Lear
made the form popular in the nineteenth century. Limerick is a town in Ireland but the name of the verse is probably derived from a Victorian custom of singing nonsense songs at parties where 'Will you come up to Limerick' was a common refrain. An example is:

> There once was a man from Nantucket
> Who kept all his cash in a bucket;
>> But his daughter named Nan
>> Ran away with a man,
> And as for the bucket, Nantucket.

lingua franca refers to 'a language adopted as a common language by speakers whose mother tongues or native languages are different'. This enables people to have a common medium of communication for various purposes, such as trading. Examples include Swahili in East Africa, Hausa in West Africa and Tok Pisin in Papua New Guinea. The term historically referred to 'a language that was a mixture of Italian, French, Greek, Spanish and Arabic, used for trading and military purposes.'

linguistics refers to the systematic, scientific study of language. It describes language and seeks to establish general principles rather than to prescribe rules of correctness.

line-break refers to the division of a word at the end of a line for space purposes. This is marked by a 'hyphen'. *See* HYPHEN.

linking adverbs and **linking adverbials** refer to words and phrases which indicate some kind of connection between one clause or sentence and another. Examples include 'however', as in 'The award had no effect on their financial situation. It did, however, have a marked effect on their morale'; 'moreover', as in 'He is an unruly pupil. Moreover, he is a bad influence on the other pupils'; 'then again', as in 'She does not have very good qualifications. Then again, most of the other candidates have even fewer'; 'in the meantime', as in 'We will not know the planning committee's decision until next week. In the meantime we can only hope'; 'instead', as in 'I thought he would have reigned. Instead he seems determined to stay'.

linking verb is a verb which 'links' a subject with its complement. Unlike other verbs, **linking verbs** do not denote an action but indicate a state. Examples of **linking verbs** include 'He is a fool', 'She appears calm', 'He appeared a sensible man', 'You seemed to become anxious', 'They became Buddhists', 'The child feels unwell', 'It is getting rather warm', 'It is growing colder', 'You look well', 'She remained loyal to her friend', 'She lived in America but remained a British citizen' and 'You seem thoughtful' and 'She seems a nice person'. **Linking verbs** are also called 'copula' or 'copular verbs'.

literary criticism refers to the formal study, discussion and evaluation of a literary work, as in 'The students who are studying literary criticism have been asked to write a critical analysis of *Ulysses* by James Joyce.'

litotes refers to a kind of understatement in which a statement is conveyed by contradicting or denying its opposite, as in 'It will be no easy task to look after their children for a week' (meaning that it will be a difficult task), 'She's not exactly communicative' (meaning she is silent or reserved).

loanword refers to a word that has been taken into another language from another. From the point of view of the language taking the word in, the word is known as a 'borrowing'—*see* BORROWING. Some **loanwords** become naturalized or fully integrated into the language and have a pronunciation and spelling reflecting the conventions of the language which has borrowed it. Other **loanwords** retain the spelling and pronunciation of the language from which they have been borrowed. These include 'Gastarbeiter', borrowed from German and meaning 'a foreign worker'.

localism refers to a word or expression whose use is restricted to a particular place or area. The area in question can be quite small, unlike 'dialect' words or 'regionalism'.

lower-case letter is the opposite of 'capital letter'. It is also known informally as 'small letter'. **Lower-case letters** are used for most words in the language. It is 'capital letters' which are exceptional in their use. *See* CAPITAL LETTER.

-ly is a common adverbial ending. *See* ADVERBS.

M

macro- is a prefix derived from the Greek meaning 'large in size or scope', as in 'macrobiotic', 'macrocosm', 'macroeconomics', 'macromolecular' and 'macrostructure'.

macron *see* **length mark**.

main clause refers to the principal clause in a sentence on which any 'subordinate clauses' depend for their sense. The main clause can stand alone and make some sense but the subordinate clauses cannot. In the sentence 'I left early because I wanted to catch the 6 o'clock train', 'I left early' is the principal clause and 'because I wanted to catch the 6 o'clock train' is the subordinate clause. In the sentence 'When we saw the strange man we were afraid', the main clause is 'we were afraid' and the subordinate clause is 'when we saw the strange man'. In the sentence 'Because it was late we decided to start out for home as soon as we could', the main clause is 'we decided to start out for home' and the subordinate clauses are 'because it was late' and 'as soon as we could'. A **main clause** can also be known as a 'principal clause' or an 'independent clause'.

mal- is a prefix derived from French meaning 'bad, unpleasant', as in 'malodorous', or 'imperfect, faulty', as in 'malabsorption', 'maladjusted', 'maladministration', 'malformation', 'malfunctioning', 'malnutrition', 'malpractice' and 'maltreatment'.

malapropism refers to the incorrect use of a word, often through confusion with a similar-sounding word. It often arises from someone's attempt to impress someone else with a knowledge of long words or of technical language. Examples include 'The doctor says the old man is not in possession of all his facilities'. Here 'facilities' has been wrongly used instead of 'faculties'. Another example is 'My friend lives in a computer belt'. Here 'computer' has been wrongly used instead of 'commuter'. Another example is 'Her husband's had a vivisection'. Here 'vivisection' has been used instead of 'vasectomy'. 'Ah! It's wonderful to be on terracotta again. I hate sailing'. Here 'terracotta' has been wrongly used instead of 'terra firma'. The effect of **malapropism** is often humorous. Sometimes people use it deliberately for a comic effect, as in 'He was under the affluence of incahol'.

Malapropism is called after Mrs Malaprop, a character in a play called *The Rivals* (1775), a comedy by R. B. Sheridan. Her name is derived from the French *mal à propos*, 'not apposite, inappropriate'. Some of her **malapropisms** in the play include 'She's as headstrong as an allegory on the banks of the Nile'. She has used 'allegory' wrongly instead of 'alligator'. Another of Mrs Malapropism's **malapropisms** is 'Illiterate him quite from your mind'. Here she has used 'illiterate' wrongly instead of 'obliterate'.

major sentence can be used to refer to a sentence that contains at least one subject and a finite verb, as in 'We are going' and 'They won'. They frequently have more elements than this, as in 'They bought a car', 'We lost the match', 'They arrived yesterday' and 'We are going away next week'. They are sometimes described as 'regular' because they divide into certain structural patterns, a subject, finite verb, adverb or adverbial, etc. The opposite of a **major sentence** is called a 'minor sentence', 'irregular sentence' or 'fragmentary sentence'. These include interjections such as 'Ouch!' and 'How terrible'; formula expressions, such as 'Good morning' and 'Well done'; and short forms of longer expressions, as in 'Traffic diverted', 'Shop closed', 'No dogs' and 'Flooding ahead'. Such short forms could be rephrased to become 'major sentences', as in 'Traffic has been diverted because of roadworks', 'The shop is closed on Sundays', 'The owner does not allow dogs in her shop' and 'There was flooding ahead on the motorway'.

-man is used with nouns to form nouns indicating someone's job, as in 'barman', 'chairman', 'clergyman', 'coalman', 'fireman', 'policeman', 'postman', 'salesman'. In modern usage when attempts are being made to remove sexism from the language alternatives have been sought for any words ending in **-man**. Formerly, words ending in **-man** were often used whether or not the person referred to was definitely known to be a man. Different ways have been found to avoid the sexism of **-man**. 'Salesman' has been changed in many cases to 'salesperson', 'chairman' often becomes 'chairperson' or 'chair'. Similarly, 'fireman' has become 'fire-fighter' and 'policeman' frequently becomes 'police officer'. *See* -PERSON.

-mania is a suffix indicating abnormal or obsessional behaviour, as in 'kleptomania', 'nymphomania' and 'pyromania'.

manner, adverbs of *see* **adverb**.

manner, adverbial clause of *see* **adverbial clause**.

masculine in grammatical terms refers to one of the grammatical genders that nouns are divided into. Nouns in the **masculine** gender include words that obviously belong to the male sex, as in 'man', 'boy', 'king', 'prince' 'bridegroom', 'schoolboy' and 'salesman'. Many words now considered to be 'of dual gender' formerly were assumed to be masculine. These include such words as 'author', 'sculptor' and 'engineer'. *See* GENDER. Gender also applies to personal pronouns and the third personal singular pronoun masculine is 'he' (subject), 'him' (object) and 'his' (possessive). For further information *see* HE; SHE.

mass noun is the same as UNCOUNTABLE NOUN.

-mate is a suffix referring to 'someone who shares something with someone', as in 'bedmate', 'classmate', 'room-mate', 'schoolmate', 'shipmate', 'team-mate' and 'workmate'.

mega- is a prefix derived from Greek meaning 'very large', as in 'megabid', 'megabucks', 'megaproduction' and 'megastar'. Many words using **mega-** in this way are modern and many of them are also informal or slang. In technical language **mega-** means 'a million times bigger than the unit to which it is attached, as in 'megabyte', 'megacycle', 'megahertz' and 'megawatt'.

meiosis is a figure of speech using understatement to emphasize the size or importance of something, as in 'He's a decent enough bloke' and 'He's rather a decent tennis player'.

melted and **molten** are liable to be confused. **Melted** is the past tense and past participle of the verb 'to melt', as in 'The chocolate melted in the heat' and 'The ice cream had melted by the time they got home'. **Melted** is also used as an adjective, as in 'melted chocolate'. **Molten** is used only as an adjective but it is not synonymous with **melted**. It means 'melted or made liquid at high temperatures', as in 'molten lava' and 'molten metal'.

meta- is a prefix derived from Greek indicating 'alteration or transformation', as in 'metamorphosis', 'metaphor' and 'metaphysics'.

metaphor is a figure of speech which compares two things by saying that one thing is another, as in 'He was a lion in the fight' (meaning that he was as brave as a lion), 'She is a mouse whenever he is present' (meaning that she is very timid), 'He is a giant among men' (meaning that he is a great man), 'She was a shining light to us all' (meaning she was a source of inspiration) and 'Life was not a bed of roses' (meaning life was not easy and enjoyable). By extension, **metaphor** refers to a word or phrase used in a sentence where it does not have a literal meaning, as in 'a butter mountain', 'a wine lake', 'My colleague is a snake in the grass', 'She always sits on the fence at committee meetings', They walked home with leaden feet' and 'He was rooted to the spot when he saw the man with the gun'. *See* MIXED METAPHOR and SIMILE.

-meter is a suffix indicating 'a measuring instrument', as in 'altimeter', 'barometer', 'pedometer', 'calorimeter', 'speedometer', 'thermometer'.

metonym is a figure of speech in which a word or expression is used to indicate something with which it has a close relationship, as in 'The position of the Crown is more uncertain than it was formerly' (meaning that the position of the monarchy is not as stable as it once was), 'The City is nervously awaiting the announcement of this month's trade figures' (meaning that the people who work in London's financial sector are nervously awaiting the announcement of this month's trade figures) and 'The Kremlin began to adopt a more enlightened approach to foreign visitors' (meaning that the Russian government began to adopt a more enlightened approach to foreign visitors), 'The White house has yet to comment on the proposal' (meaning that the President of the United States has yet to reply to the proposal).

-metre is a suffix indicating 'meter, the unit of length', as in 'centimetre', 'kilometre' and 'millimetre'.

micro- is a prefix derived from Greek meaning 'very

small', as in 'microbiology', 'microfiche', 'microfilm', 'microscope', 'microsurgery'.

milli- is a prefix derived from Latin meaning 'thousand', as in 'millisecond'.

mini- is a prefix derived from Latin meaning 'very small, least', as in 'minimum', 'minimal', and 'miniature'. **Mini-** is frequently used to form modern words, as in 'minibus', 'minicab', 'mini-computer', 'mini-cruise', 'mini-golf', 'mini-market' and 'miniskirt'. Modern words beginning with **mini-** can be spelt either with a hyphen or without.

minor sentence *see* **major sentence**.

mis- is a prefix indicating 'badly, wrongly', as in 'misbehave', 'miscalculate', 'misdirect', 'mishandle', 'mishear', 'misjudge', 'mismanage', 'mispronounce', 'misspell', 'mistreat', 'mistrust', 'misunderstanding' and 'misuse'.

mixed metaphor occurs when unrelated metaphors are put in the same sentence. Examples include 'She sailed into the room with both guns blazing'. Here the use of the word 'sail' belongs to nautical metaphors but the 'guns blazing' belongs to cowboy or Wild West metaphors. Another example is 'The company's new flagship did not get off the ground'. Here 'flagship' is a nautical term and 'get off the ground' refers to aircraft'. Another example is 'They were caught red-handed with their trousers down'. Here 'caught red-handed' is a metaphorical reference to a murderer caught with blood on his/her hands but 'caught with one's trousers down' is either a reference to the embarrassing experience of being caught unawares in the toilet or else caught in an embarrassing sexual situation.

modifier refers to a word, or group of words, that 'modifies' or affects the meaning of another word in some way, usually by adding more information about it. **Modifiers** are frequently used with nouns. They can be adjectives, as in 'He works in the *main* building' and 'They need a *larger* house'. **Modifiers** of nouns can be nouns themselves, as in 'the *theatre* profession', 'the *publishing* industry' and '*singing* tuition'. They can also be place names, as in 'the *Edinburgh* train', 'a *Paris* cafe' and 'the *London* underground' or adverbs of place and direction, as in 'a *downstairs* cloakroom' and 'an *upstairs* sitting room.

Adverbs, adjectives and pronouns can be accompanied by **modifiers.** Examples of modifiers with adverbs include 'walking *amazingly* quickly' and 'stopping *incredibly* abruptly'. Examples of modifiers with adjectives include 'a *really* warm day' and 'a *deliriously* happy child'. Examples of modifiers with pronouns include '*almost* no one there' and '*practically* everyone present'.

The examples given above are all 'pre-modifiers'. *See also* POST-MODIFIER.

-monger is a suffix derived from Old English meaning 'dealer, trader', as in 'fishmonger' and 'ironmonger'. As well as being used for occupations in which people sell things, it is used for people who 'trade' in less tangible things, as in 'gossipmonger', 'rumourmonger', 'scaremonger' and 'warmonger'.

mono- is a prefix derived from Greek meaning 'one, single', as in 'monochrome', 'monocracy', 'monogamy', 'monologue', 'monoplane', 'monosyllabic' and 'monoxide'.

months of the year are spelt with initial capital letters, as in January, February, March, April, May, June, July, August, September, October, November and December.

modal verb refers to a type of 'auxiliary verb' that 'helps' the main verb to express a range of meanings including, for example, such meanings as possibility, probability, wants, wishes, necessity, permission, suggestions, etc. The main modal verbs are 'can', 'could'; 'may', 'might'; 'will', 'would'; 'shall', 'should'; 'must'. Modal verbs have only one form. They have no -*s* form in the third person singular, no infinitive and no participles. Examples of modal verbs include 'He cannot read and write', 'She could go if she wanted to' (expressing ability); 'You can have another biscuit', 'You may answer the question' (expressing permission); 'We may see her on the way to the station', 'We might get there by nightfall' (expressing possibility); 'Will you have some wine?', 'Would you take a seat?' (expressing an offer or invitation); 'We should arrive by dawn', 'That must be a record' (expressing probability and certainty); 'You may prefer to wait', 'You might like to leave instructions' (expressing suggestion); 'Can you find the time to phone him for me?' ,'Could you give him a message?' (expressing instructions and requests); 'They must leave at once', 'We must get there on time' (expressing necessity).

mood refers to one of the categories into which verbs are divided. The verb moods are 'indicative', 'imperative' and 'subjunctive'. The indicative makes a statement, as in 'He lives in France', 'They have two children' and 'It's starting to rain'. The 'imperative' is used for giving orders or making requests, as in 'Shut that door!', 'Sit quietly until the teacher arrives' and 'Please bring me some coffee'. The subjunctive was originally a term in Latin grammar and expressed a wish, supposition, doubt, improbability or other non-factual statement. It is used in English for hypothetical statements and certain formal 'that' clauses, as in 'If I were you I would have nothing to do with it', 'If you were to go now you would arrive on time', 'Someone suggested that we ask for more money' and 'It was his solicitor who suggested that he sue the firm'. The word **mood** arose because it was said to indicate the verb's attitude or viewpoint. *See* SUBJUNCTIVE.

more is an adverb which is added to some adjectives to make the comparative form. In general it is the longer adjectives which have **more** as part of their comparative form, as in 'more abundant', 'more beautiful', 'more catastrophic', 'more dangerous', 'more elegant', 'more frantic', 'more graceful', 'more handsome', 'more intelligent', 'more luxurious', 'more manageable', 'more noteworthy', 'more opulent', 'more precious', 'more ravishing', 'more satisfactory', 'more talented', 'more unusual', 'more valuable'. Examples of adverbs with **more** in their comparative form include 'more elegantly', 'more gracefully', 'more energetically', 'more dangerously' and 'more determinedly'. *See* COMPARISON OF ADJECTIVES.

most is an adverb added to some adjectives and adverbs to make the superlative form. In general it is the longer adjectives which have **most** as part of their superlative form, as in 'most abundant', 'most beautiful', 'most catastrophic', 'most dangerous', 'most elegant', 'most frantic', 'most graceful', 'most handsome', 'most intelligent', 'most luxurious', 'most manageable', 'most noteworthy', 'most opulent', 'most precious', most ravishing', 'most satisfactory', 'most talented', 'most unusual', 'most valuable'. Examples of adverbs with **most** in their superlative form include 'most elegantly', 'most gracefully', 'most energetically', 'most dangerously' and 'most determinedly'.

mother tongue refers to the language that one first learns, the language of which one is a 'native speaker'. It means the same as 'native tongue'.

ms, miss and miss *see* **letter-writing.**

mow has two possible past participles—**mowed and mown,** as in 'He has not yet mowed the grass' and 'We have mown the grass several times this summer'. The two participles are interchangeable. Only **mowed,** however, can be used as the past tense, as in 'They mowed the grass yesterday' and 'If they mowed the grass more often the garden would be tidier'. **Mown** can also be an adjective, as in 'the smell of freshly mown hay'.

multi- is a prefix derived from Latin meaning 'many many', as in 'multiply', 'multitude' and 'multitudinous'. **Multi-** is frequently used to form new modern words, as in 'multi-married', 'multi-media', 'multi-publicized', 'multi-purpose', 'multi-storey ', 'multi-talented' and 'multi-travelled'.

multi-sentence refers to a sentence with more than one clause, as in 'She tripped over a rock and broke her ankle' and 'She was afraid when she saw the strange man'.

N

-naut is a suffix derived from Greek 'sailor' and meaning 'navigator', as in 'astronaut' and 'cosmonaut'.

negative sentence refers to a sentence that is the opposite of 'positive sentence'. 'She has a dog' is an example of a positive sentence. 'She does not have a dog' is an example of a **negative sentence**. The **negative** concept is expressed by an 'auxiliary' verb accompanied by 'not' or 'n't'. Other words used in **negative sentences** include 'never', 'nothing' and 'by no means', as in 'She has never been here' and 'We heard nothing'.

neither as an adjective or a pronoun takes a singular verb, as in 'Neither parent will come' and 'Neither of them wishes to come'. In the **neither ... nor** construction, a singular verb is used if both parts of the construction are singular, as in 'Neither Jane nor Mary was present'. If both parts are plural the verb is plural, as in 'Neither their parents nor their grandparents are willing to look after them'. If the construction involves a mixture of singular and plural, the verb traditionally agrees with the subject that is nearest it, as in 'Neither her mother nor her grandparents are going to come' and 'Neither her grandparents nor her mother is going to come'. If pronouns are used, the nearer one governs the verb as in 'Neither they nor he is at fault' and 'Neither he nor they are at fault'.

neologism refers to a word that has been newly coined or newly introduced into the language, as 'camcorder', 'Jacuzzi' and 'karaoke'.

neuro- is a prefix derived from Greek meaning 'nerve', as in 'neuritis', 'neurology', 'neuron' and 'neurosurgery'.

neuter refers to one of the grammatical genders. The other two grammatical genders are 'masculine' and 'feminine'. Inanimate objects are members of the **neuter** gender. Examples include 'table', 'desk', 'garden', 'spade', 'flower' and 'bottle'.

non-finite clause is a clause which contains a 'non-finite verb'. Thus in the sentence 'He works hard to earn a living', 'to earn a living' is a non-finite clause since 'to earn' is an infinitive and so a non-finite verb. Similarly in the sentence 'Getting there was a problem', 'getting there' is a non-finite clause, 'getting' being a present participle and so a non-finite verb.

non-finite verb is one which shows no variation in tense and which has no subject. The non-finite verb forms include the infinitive form, as in 'go', the present participle and gerund, as in 'going', and the past participle, as in 'gone'.

noun indicates the name of something or someone. Thus 'anchor', 'baker', 'cat', 'elephant', 'foot', 'gate', 'lake', 'pear', 'shoe', 'trunk' and 'wallet' are all nouns. There are various categories of nouns. *See* ABSTRACT NOUN, COMMON NOUN, CONCRETE NOUN, COUNTABLE NOUN, PROPER NOUN and UNCOUNTABLE NOUN.

noun clause refers to a 'subordinate clause' which performs a function in a sentence similar to a noun or noun phrase. It can act as the subject, object or complement of a main clause. In the sentence 'Where he goes is his own business', 'where he goes' is a **noun clause**. In the sentence 'They asked why he objected', 'why he objected' is a **noun clause**. A **noun clause** is also known as a **nominal clause**.

noun phrase refers to a group of words containing a noun as its main word and functioning like a noun in a sentence. Thus it can function as the subject, object or complement of a sentence. In the sentence 'The large black dog bit him', 'the large black dog' is a **noun phrase** and in the sentence 'They bought a house with a garden', 'with a garden' is a **noun phrase**. In the sentence 'She is a complete fool', 'a complete fool' is a noun phrase.

number in grammar is a classification consisting of 'singular' and 'plural'. Thus the **number** of the pronoun 'they' is 'plural' and the **number** of the verb 'carries' is singular. *See* NUMBER AGREEMENT.

number agreement or **concord** refers to the fact that grammatical units should agree in terms of number. Thus a singular subject is followed by a singular verb, as in 'The girl likes flowers', 'He hates work' and 'She was carrying a suitcase'. Similarly a plural subject should be followed by a plural verb, as in 'They have many problems', 'The men work hard' and 'The girls are training hard'.

numbers can be written in either figures or words. It is largely a matter of taste which method is adopted. As long as the method is consistent it does not really matter. Some establishments, such as a publishing house or a newspaper office, will have a house style. For example, some of them prefer to have numbers up to 10 written in words, as in 'They have two boys and three girls'. If this system is adopted, guidance should be sought as to whether a mixture of figures and words in the same sentence is acceptable, as in 'We have 12 cups but only six saucers', or whether the rule should be broken in such situations as 'We have twelve cups but only six saucers'.

numeral is a word for 'number', as in 'print all the numerals in bold type'. **Numeral** is often used to refer to 'one, two, three, etc' in grammar since **number** is used to refer to the singular/plural category.

O

object refers to the part of a sentence that is acted upon or is affected by the verb. It usually follows the verb to which it relates. There are two forms of **object**—the 'direct object' and 'indirect object'. A direct object can be a noun, and in the sentence 'The girl hit the ball', 'ball' is a noun and the object. In the sentence 'They bought a house', 'house' is a noun and the object. In the sentence 'They made an error', 'error' is a noun and the object. A direct object can be a noun phrase, and in the sentence 'He has bought a large house', 'a large house' is a noun phrase and the object. In the sentence 'She loves the little girl', 'the little girl' is a noun phrase and the object. In the sentence 'They both wear black clothes', 'black clothes' is a noun phrase and the object'. A direct object can be a noun clause, and in the sentence 'I know what he means', 'what he means' is a noun phrase and the object. In the sentence 'He denied that he had been involved', 'that he had been involved' is a noun phrase and the object. In the sentence 'I asked when he would return', 'when he would return' is a noun phrase and the object. A direct object can also be a pronoun, and in the sentence 'She hit him', 'him' is a pronoun and the object. In the sentence 'They had a car but they sold it', 'it' is a pronoun and the object. In the sentence 'She loves them', 'them' is a pronoun and the object. *See* INDIRECT OBJECT.

objective case is the case expressing the 'object'. In Latin it is known as the 'accusative' case.

oblique is a diagonal mark / which has various uses. Its principal use is to show alternatives, as in 'he/she', 'Dear Sir/Madam', 'two/three-room flat' and 'the budget for 1993/4'. The **oblique** is used in some abbreviations, as in ' c/o Smith' (meaning 'care of Smith'). The word 'per' is usually shown by means of an **oblique**, as in 60km/hr (60 kilometres per hour).

officialese is a derogatory term for the vocabulary and style of writing often found in official reports and documents and thought of as being pretentious and difficult to understand. It is usually considered to be the prime example of GOBBLEDEGOOK.

-oholic *see* **-aholic**.

-ology is a suffix derived from Greek indicating 'study of', as in 'biology', 'geology' and 'technology'.

omni- is a prefix derived from Latin indicating 'all', as in 'omnipotent' and 'omnivorous'.

onomatopoeia is a figure of speech which uses words whose sound suggests their meaning, as in 'The sausages sizzled in the pan', 'The fire crackled in the grate' and 'The water gurgled in the pipes'.

orthographic refers to spelling, as in 'words which give rise to orthographic problems'.

orthography means the study or science of how words are spelt, as in 'make a survey of the orthography and the pronunciation of Scandinavian languages'.

ordinal numbers refer to 'first', 'second', 'third', etc, as opposed to 'cardinal numbers' which are 'one', 'two, 'three', etc.

-osis is a suffix derived from Greek indicating either 'a disease', as in 'cirrhosis' and 'thrombosis'.

oxymoron is a figure of speech which is based on the linking of incongruous or contradictory words, as in 'and honour rooted in dishonour stood' (Tennyson) and 'the wisest fool in Christendom'.

P

paragraph is a subdivision of a piece of prose. Many people find it difficult to divide their work into paragraphs. Learning to do so can be difficult but it is an area of style that improves with practice and writers develop an intuition as when to start a new paragraph.

A **paragraph** should deal with one particular theme or point of the writer's writing or argument. When that has been dealt with, a new paragraph should be started.

However, there are other considerations to be taken into account. If the paragraph is very long it can appear offputting visually to the would-be reader and can be difficult to make one's way through as a reader. In such cases it is best to sub-divide one's themes and shorten one's paragraphs.

On the other hand it is best not to make all of one's paragraphs too short or this can create a disjointed, rather staccato effect which might well not be intended. It is best to try to aim for a mixture of lengths to create some variety in one's writing and to tempt one's potential readers to read on.

Traditionally it was frowned upon to have a one-sentence paragraph but there are no hard and fast rules about this. Usually it takes more than one sentence to develop the theme of the paragraph, unless one is a tabloid journalist or copywriter for an advertising firm, and it is best to avoid long, complex sentences.

The opening paragraph of a piece of writing should introduce the topic about which one is writing. The closing paragraph should sum up what one has been writing about. New paragraphs begin on new lines and they are usually indented from the margin. In the case of dialogue in a work of fiction, each speaker's utterance usually begins on a new line for the clarification of the reader.

parenthesis *see* **brackets**.

passive voice designates the voice of a verb whereby the subject is the recipient of the action of the verb. Thus, in the sentence 'Mary was kicked by her brother', 'Mary' is the receiver of the 'kick' and so 'kick' is in the passive voice. Similarly, in the sentence 'James was hit by the ball', 'James' is the receiver of the 'hit' and so 'hit' is in the passive voice. Had the former sentence been in the active voice it would have been 'Her brother kicked Mary'. In this sentence 'the brother' is the subject and not the receiver of the action.

past participles are formed by adding *-ed* or *-d* to the base words of regular verbs, as in 'acted', ' alluded', 'boarded', 'dashed', 'flouted', 'handed', 'loathed', 'tended' and 'wanted', or in various other ways for irregular verbs. *See* IRREGULAR VERBS.

past tense is formed by adding *-ed* or *-d* to the base form of the verb in regular verbs, as in 'added', 'crashed', 'graded', 'smiled', 'rested' and 'yielded', and in various ways for irregular verbs. *See* IRREGULAR VERBS and TENSE.

perfect tense *see* **tense**.

period *see* **full stop**.

personal pronouns are used to refer back to someone or something that has already been mentioned. The personal pronouns are divided into subject pronouns, object , pronouns and possessive pronouns They are also categorized according to 'person'. *See* FIRST PERSON, SECOND PERSON and THIRD PERSON.

plural noun refers to 'more than one' and is contrasted with 'singular noun'. Singular nouns form plural forms in different ways. Most singular nouns add *s*, as in 'bat/ bats', 'monkey/monkeys', 'table/tables', 'umbrella/umbrellas', or add *es*, as in 'church/churches' or 'torch/ torches'. Singular nouns ending in a consonant followed by *y* add *ies*, as in 'fairy/fairies' and 'story/stories'. Some plural forms are formed irregularly. *See* IRREGULAR PLURALS.

possessive apostrophe *see* **apostrophe**.

possessive pronoun *see* **personal pronoun, first person, second person** and **third person**.

postmodifiers come after the main word of a noun phrase, as in 'of stone' in 'tablets of stone'.

predicate refers to all the parts of a clause or sentence that are not contained in the subject. Thus in the sentence 'The little girl was exhausted and hungry', 'exhausted and hungry' is the **predicate**. Similarly, in the sentence 'The tired old man slept like a top', 'slept like a top' is the **predicate**.

predicative adjectives help to form the predicate and so come after the verb, as 'tired' in 'She was very tired' and 'mournful' in 'The music was very mournful'.

premodifiers come before the main word of a noun phrase, as 'green' in 'green dress' and 'pretty' in 'pretty houses'.

prepositions are words which relate two elements of a sentence, clause or phrase together. They show how the elements relate in time or space and generally precede the words which they 'govern'. Words governed by **prepositions** are nouns or pronouns. **Prepositions** are often very short words, as 'at', 'in', 'on', 'to', 'before' and 'after'. Some complex prepositions consist of two words, as 'ahead of', 'instead of', 'apart from', and some consist of three, as 'with reference to', 'in accordance with' and 'in addition to'. Examples of **prepositions** in sentences include 'The cat sat on the mat', 'We were at a concert', 'They are in shock', 'We are going to France', 'She arrived before me', 'Apart from you she has no friends' and 'We acted in accordance with your instructions'.

present continuous *see* tense.

present participle *see* -ing words.

present tense *see* tense.

pronoun is a word that takes the place of a noun or a noun phrase. *See* PERSONAL PRONOUNS, HE, HER, HIM and HIS, RECIPROCAL PRONOUNS, REFLEXIVE PRONOUNS, DEMONSTRATIVE PRONOUNS, RELATIVE PRONOUNS, DISTRIBUTIVE PRONOUNS,

INDEFINITE PRONOUNS and INTERROGATIVE PRONOUNS.

proper noun is a noun which refers to a particular individual or specific thing. It is the 'name' of someone or something', as in Australia, Vesuvius, John Brown, River Thames, Rome and Atlantic Ocean. *See* CAPITAL LETTERS.

Q

question mark refers to the punctuation mark that is placed at the end of a question or interrogative sentence, as in 'Who is he?', 'Where are they?', 'Why have they gone?', 'Whereabouts are they?', 'When are you going?' and 'What did he say?'. The **question mark** is sometimes known as the 'query'.

question tag refers to a phrase that is interrogative in form but is not really asking a question. It is added to a statement to seek agreement, etc. Examples include 'That was a lovely meal, wasn't it?', 'You will be able to go, won't you?', 'He's not going to move house, is he?' and 'She doesn't drive, does she?'. Sentences containing **question tags** have 'question marks' at the end.

query *see* **question mark**.

quotation marks, also known as 'inverted commas' or 'quotes', are used in 'direct speech'. For the use of **quotation marks** in 'direct speech' *see* DIRECT SPEECH. **Quotation marks** are also used to enclose titles of newspapers, books, plays, films, musical works and works of art, as in 'The Times', 'Animal Farm', 'Othello', 'My Fair Lady' and 'Portrait of the Artist'. **Quotation marks** may consist of a set of single inverted comas or a set of double inverted commas. If a title, etc, is to be enclosed in quotation marks and the title is part of a piece of writing already in quotation marks for some other reason, such as being part of direct speech, then the quotation marks round the title should be in the type of quotation marks opposite to the other ones. Thus if the piece of writing is in single quotation marks then the title should be in double quotation marks. If the piece of prose is in double quotation marks the title should be in single quotation marks. Examples include 'Have you read "Wuthering Heights"?' and "Did you go to see 'My Fair Lady'?"

quotes *see* **quotation marks**.

R

re- is a common prefix, meaning 'again', in verbs. In most cases it is not followed by a hyphen, as in 'retrace one's footsteps', 'a retrial ordered by the judge' and 'reconsider his decision'. However, it should be followed by a hyphen if its absence is likely to lead to confusion with another word, as in 're-cover a chair'/'recover from an illness', 're-count the votes'/'recount a tale of woe', 'the re-creation of a 17th-century village for a film set'/'play tennis for recreation' and 're-form the group'/'reform the prison system'. In cases where the second element of a word begins with *e*, **re-** is traditionally followed by a hyphen, as in 're-educate', 're-entry' and 're-echo', but in modern usage the hyphen is frequently omitted.

reciprocal pronoun is used to convey the idea of reciprocity or a two-way relationship. The **reciprocal pronouns** are 'each other' and 'one another'. Examples include 'They don't love each other any more', 'They seem to hate each other', 'We must try to help each other', 'The children were calling one another names', 'The two families were always criticizing one another' and 'The members of the family blame one another for their mother's death'.

reduplication refers to the process by which words are created by repetition or by semi-repetition. These include 'argy-bargy', 'dilly-dally', 'shilly-shally', 'flimflam', 'heebie-jeebies', 'hocus-pocus', 'hugger-mugger', 'knick-knack', and 'mish-mash'.

reflexive pronoun is one which refers back to a noun or pronoun which has occurred earlier in the same sentence. The **reflexive pronouns** include 'myself', 'ourselves'; 'yourself', 'yourselves'; 'himself', 'herself', 'itself', 'themselves'. Examples include 'The children washed themselves', 'He cut himself shaving', 'Have you hurt yourself?' and 'She has cured herself of the habit'.

Reflexive pronouns are sometimes used for emphasis, as in 'The town itself was not very interesting' and 'The headmaster himself punished the boys'. They can also be used to indicate that something has been done by somebody by his/her own efforts without any help, as in 'He built the house himself', 'We converted the attic ourselves'. They can also indicate that someone or something is alone, as in 'She lives by herself' and 'The house stands by itself'.

regular verb see **irregular verb**.

relative clause is a subordinate clause which has the function of an adjective. It is introduced by a **relative pronoun.** *See* RELATIVE PRONOUNS.

relative pronouns introduce **relative clauses**. The **relative pronouns** are 'who', 'whom', 'whose', 'which' and 'that'. Examples of **relative clauses** introduced by **relative pronouns** include 'There is the man who stole the money', 'She is the person to whom I gave the money', 'This is the man whose wife won the prize', 'They criticized the work which he had done' and 'That's the house that I would like to buy'. **Relative pronouns** refer back to a noun or noun phrase in the main clause. These nouns and noun phrases are known as 'antecedents'. The antecedents in the example sentences are respectively 'man', 'person', 'man', 'work' and 'house'.

Sometimes the **relative clause** divides the parts of the main clause, as in 'The woman whose daughter is ill is very upset', 'The people whom we met on holiday were French' and 'The house that we liked best was too expensive'.

reported speech *see* **indirect speech**.

retro- is a prefix derived from Latin meaning 'back, backwards', as in 'retrograde', 'retrospect', 'retrorocket'.

retronym is a word or phrase that has had to be renamed slightly in the light of another invention, etc. For example, an ordinary guitar has become 'acoustic guitar' because of the existence of 'electric guitar'. Leather has sometimes become 'real leather' because of the existence of 'imitation leather'.

rhetorical question is a question which is asked to achieve some kind of effect and requires no answer. Examples include 'What's this country coming to?', 'Did you ever see the like', 'Why do these things happen to me?', 'Where did youth go?', 'Death, where is thy sting?' and 'Where does time go?'.

root means the same as **base**.

S

second person refers to the person or thing to whom one is talking. The term is applied to personal pronouns. The second person singular whether acting as the subject of a sentence is 'you', as in 'I told you so', 'We informed you of our decision' and 'They might have asked you sooner'. The **second person** personal pronoun does not alter its form in the plural in English, unlike in some languages. The possessive form of the **second person** pronoun is 'yours' whether singular or plural, as in "He said to the boys 'These books are not yours'" and 'This pen must be yours'.

semi-colon is rather a rare and also rather formal form of punctuation. It is mainly used between clauses that are not joined by any form of conjunction, as in 'We had a wonderful holiday; sadly they did not', 'The children are tired; they are also hungry'. 'She was my sister; she was also my best friend' and 'He was a marvellous friend; he is much missed'. A dash is sometimes used instead of a semi-colon but this more informal.

The **semi-colon** is also used to form subsets in a long list or series of names so that the said list seems less complex, as in 'The young man who wants to be a journalist has applied everywhere. He has applied to *The Times* in London; *The Washington Post* in Washington; *The Globe and Mail* in Toronto; *The Age* in Melbourne; *The Tribune* in Chicago.

The **semi-colon** is also sometimes used before 'however', 'nevertheless' 'hence', etc, as in 'He comes from Scotland; hence his nickname of Jock', 'We have extra seats for the concert; however you must not feel obliged to come'.

sentence is at the head of the hierarchy of grammar. All the other elements, such as words, phrases and clauses go to make up sentences. It is difficult to define a sentence. In terms of recognizing a sentence visually it can be described as beginning with a capital letter and ending with a full stop, or with an equivalent to the full stop, such as an exclamation mark. One suggested definition is that it is 'the complete expression of a single thought' but this seems rather a philosophical definition. Perhaps all one can say is that a sentence is a unit of grammar that can stand alone and make sense and obeys certain grammatical rules, such as usually having a subject and a predicate, as in 'The girl banged the door', where 'the girl' is the 'subject' and 'the door' is the predicate. *See* MAJOR SENTENCE, SIMPLE SENTENCE, COMPLEX SENTENCE.

simile is a figure of speech in which something is compared with another and said to be like it. This is in contradistinction to 'metaphor' where one thing is said actually to be another. Examples of similes include 'She is like an angel', 'Her hair is like silk', Her eyes are like forget-me-nots. 'The old man's skin is like leather', He swims like a fish'.

simple sentence is a sentence which cannot be broken down into other causes. It generally contains a finite verb. Simple sentences include 'The man stole the car', 'She nudged him' and 'He kicked the ball. See COMPLEX SENTENCE and COMPOUND SENTENCE.

sexism was formerly widespread in the English language whether this was intentional or not. Efforts are now being made to rectify this situation, although some of the suggestions made are rather extreme. These suggestions include 'herstory' for 'history' and the replacement of man by person ludicrous degree, as 'personhole' for 'manhole'. Most of these rather extreme ideas have not gained widespread currency. Sensible progress has, however, been made. *See* HE; EACH; -MAN and -PERSON.

singular noun refers to 'one' rather than 'more than one', which is the plural form. *See* PLURAL; IRREGULAR PLURAL.

spelling *see* **Appendix I**.

split infinitive refers to an infinitive which has had another word in the form of an adverb, placed between itself and 'to', as in 'to rudely push' and 'to quietly leave'. This was once considered a a great grammatical sin but the **split infinitive** is becoming acceptable in modern usage. In any case it sometimes makes for a clumsy sentence if one slavishly adheres to the correct form.

spoonerism refers to the accidental or deliberate transposition of the initial letters of two or more words, as in 'the queer old dean' instead of 'the dear old queen', 'a blushing crow' instead of a 'crushing blow' and 'a well-boiled icicle' instead of a 'well-oiled bicycle'. **Spoonerism** is called after the Reverend William Archibald Spooner (1844–1930) of Oxford University.

stative present *see* **tense**.

strong verb is the more common term for 'irregular verb'. *See* IRREGULAR VERB.

subject of a sentence or clause is usually either a noun, as in 'Birds fly' (birds is the noun as subject); a noun phrase, as in 'The people in the town dislike him' (the people in the town' is the subject); a pronoun, as in 'She hit the child' (she is the pronoun as subject); a proper noun, as in 'Paris is the capital of France'. *See* DUMMY SUBJECT.

subjunctive *see* **mood**.

subordinate clause is dependent on another clause, namely the 'main' clause. Unlike the main clause, it cannot stand alone and make sense. **Subordinate clauses** are introduced by conjunctions. Examples of conjunctions which introduce subordinate clauses include 'after', 'before', 'when', 'if', 'because' and 'since'. *See* ADVERBIAL CLAUSE; NOUN CLAUSE.

suffix is an 'affix' which goes at the beginning of a word. 'Pre-' is a suffix in 'prepare' and 'pre-holiday'. *See* AFFIX.

superlative forms of of adjectives and adverbs follow the same rules as comparative forms, except that they end in *-est* instead of *-er* and the longer ones use 'most' instead of 'more'.

syllepsis is another word for **zeugma**.

synecdoche is a figure of speech in which the part is put for the whole. For example 'The power of the Sceptre is fading' where sceptre is used for 'monarch'. 'The country has a fleet of a hundred sail' where 'sail' is used for 'ship'. 'He had a very successful career on the boards' where 'boards' is used for 'stage'.

T

tautology refers to unnecessary repetition, as in 'new innovations', 'a see-through transparent material' and 'one after the other in succession'.

techno- is a prefix derived from Greek meaning 'craft, skill', as in 'technical', 'technology', 'technique' and 'technocrat'.

tele- is a prefix derived from Greek meaning 'distance' as in 'telegraph', 'telephone', 'telescope' and 'television'.

tense is used to show the time at which the action of a verb takes place. One of the tenses in English is the 'present tense'. It is used to indicate an action now going on or a state now existing. A distinction can be made between the 'habitual present', which marks habitual or repeated actions or recurring events, and the 'stative present', which indicates something that is true at all times. Examples of 'habitual present' include 'He works long hours' and 'She walks to work'. Examples of the 'stative tense' include 'The world is round' and 'Everyone must die eventually'.

The 'progressive present' or 'continuous present' is formed with the verb 'to be' and the 'present participle', as in ,He is walking to the next village', 'They are thinking about leaving' , 'She was driving along the road when she saw him' and 'They were worrying about the state of the economy'

The 'past tense' refers to an action or state which has taken place before the present time. In the case of 'irregular verbs' it is formed by adding *-ed* to the base form of the verb, as in 'fear/feared', 'look/looked', and 'turn/turned'. For the past tense of 'irregular verbs', *see* IRREGULAR VERBS.

The 'future tense' refers to an action or state that will take place at some time in the future. It is formed with 'will' and 'shall'. Traditionally 'will' was used with the second and third person pronouns ('you', 'he/she/it', 'they') and 'shall' with the first person ('I' and 'we'), as in 'You will be bored', 'He will soon be home', 'They will leave tomorrow', 'I shall buy some bread' and 'We shall go by train'. Also traditionally, 'shall' was used with the second and third persons to indicate emphasis, insistence, determination, refusal, etc, as in 'You shall go to the ball' and 'He shall not be admitted'. 'Will' was used with the first person in the same way, as in 'I will get even with him' and 'We will get our money back'.

In modern usage 'will' is generally used for the first person as well as for second and third, as in 'I will see you tomorrow' and 'We will be there soon' and 'shall' is used for emphasis, insistence, etc, for first, second and third persons.

The 'future tense' can also be formed with the use of 'be about to' or 'be going to', as in 'We were about to leave' and 'They were going to look for somewhere to live'.

Other tenses include the 'perfect tense' which is formed using the verb 'to have' and the past participle. In the case of 'regular verbs' the 'past participle' is formed by adding *-ed* to the base form of the verb. For the past participles of 'irregular verbs', *see* IRREGULAR VERBS. Examples of the 'perfect tense' include 'He has played his last match', 'We have travelled all day' and 'They have thought a lot about it'.

The 'past perfect tense' or 'pluperfect tense' is formed using the verb 'to have' and the past participle, as in 'She had no idea that he was dead', 'We had worked as hard as possible' and 'They had felt unhappy about the situation'.

The 'future perfect' is formed using the verb 'to have' and the past participle, as in 'He will have arrived by now' and 'We will have been away for four years by then.'

the usually refers back to something already identified or to something specific, as in 'Where is the key?', 'What have you done with the book which I gave you?' and 'We have found the book which we lost'. It is also used to denote someone or something as being the only one, as in 'the House of Lords', 'the King of Spain' and 'the President of Russia', and to indicate a class or group, as in 'the aristocracy', the cat family' and 'the teaching profession'. **The** is sometimes pronounced 'thee' when it is used to identify someone or something unique or important, as in 'Is that the John Frame over there?' and 'She is the fashion designer of the moment'.

they *see* **he**.

third person refers to a third party not the speaker or the person or thing being spoken to. Note that 'person' in this context can refer to things as well as people. 'Person' in this sense applies to personal pronouns. The third person singular forms are 'he', 'she' and 'it' when the subject of a sentence or clause, as in 'She will win' and 'It will be fine'. The third person singular forms are 'him', 'her', 'it' when the object, as in 'His behaviour hurt her' and 'She meant it'. The third person plural is 'they' when the subject, as in 'They have left' and 'They were angry' and 'them' when the object, as in 'His words made them angry' and 'We accompanied them'.

The possessive forms of the singular are 'his', 'hers' and 'its', as in 'he played his guitar' and 'The dog hurt its leg' and the the possessive form of the plural is theirs, as in 'That car is theirs' and 'They say that the book is theirs'. *See* HE.

to-infinitive refers to the 'infinitive' form of the verb when it is accompanied by 'to' rather than when it is the 'bare infinitive' without 'to'. Examples of the **to-infinitive** include 'We were told to go', 'I didn't want to stay' and 'To get there on time we'll have to leave now'.

transitive verb is a verb which takes a 'direct object'. In the sentence 'The boy broke the window', 'window' is a 'direct object' and so 'broke' (past tense of 'break' is a transitive verb. In the sentence 'She eats fruit' 'fruit' is

trisyllabic

a 'direct object' and so 'eat' is a transitive verb. In the sentence 'They kill enemy soldiers', 'enemy soldiers' is a 'direct object' and so 'kill' is a transitive verb'. *See* DIRECT OBJECT and INTRANSITIVE VERB.

trisyllabic means having three syllables. Examples include 'monument', 'relative' and 'satisfy'.

U

ultra- is a prefix derived from Latin meaning 'beyond', as in 'ultraviolet' and 'ltramodern'.

umlaut refers to the diacritic which indicates a change of vowel sound in German, as in *mädchen*.

un- is a prefix with two meanings. It can mean either 'not', as in 'unclean', 'untrue' and 'unwise'. it can also mean 'back, reversal', as in 'undo', 'unfasten', 'unlatch' and 'untie'.

uncount noun see uncountable noun.

uncountable noun refers to a noun that is not usually pluralized or 'counted'. Such a noun is usually preceded by 'some', rather than 'a'. **Uncountable nouns** often refer to substances or commodities or qualities, processes and states. Examples of uncountable nouns include butter, china, luggage, petrol, sugar, heat, information, poverty, richness and warmth.In some situations it is possible to have a countable version of what is usually an **uncountable noun**. Thus 'sugar' is usually considered to be an 'uncountable noun' but it can be used in a 'countable' form in contexts such as 'I take two sugars in my coffee please'. Some nouns exist in an uncountable and 'countable' form. Examples include 'cake', as in 'Have some cake' and 'She ate three cakes' and 'She could not paint for lack of light' and 'the lights went out'.

uni- is a prefix derived from Latin meaning 'one', as in unicycle, unilateral and unity.

V

verb is often known as a 'doing' word. Although this is rather restrictive, since it tends to preclude auxiliary verbs, modal verbs, etc. The **verb** is the word in a sentence that is most concerned with the action and is usually essential to the structure of the sentence. Verbs 'inflect' and indicate tense, voice, mood, number, number and person. Most of the information on verbs has been placed under related entries. *See* ACTIVE, PASSIVE, VOICE, AUXILIARY VERB, MODAL VERB, MOOD, FINITE VERB, NON-FINITE VERB, TRANSITIVE VERB, INTRANSITIVE VERB, IRREGULAR VERB, LINKING VERB, -ING FORMS and PHRASAL VERBS.

verb phrase refers to a group of verb forms which has the same function as a single verb. Examples include 'have been raining', 'must have been lying', 'should not have been doing' and 'has been seen doing'.

virgule is a rare word for OBLIQUE.

vocative case is relevant mainly to languages such as Latin which are based on cases and inflections. In English the vocative is expressed by addressing someone, as in 'John, could I see you for a minute', or by some form of greeting, endearment or exclamation.

voice

voice is one of the categories that describes verbs. It involves two different ways of looking at the action of verbs. It is divided into 'active voice' and 'passive voice'. *See* ACTIVE and PASSIVE.

W

weak verb is a less common term for 'regular verb'. *See* IRREGULAR VERB.

who and **whom** *see* RELATIVE CLAUSE.

whose and **whose** are liable to be confused because they sound the same. However they are not at all the same. Who's is a contraction of 'who is' and is used in speech and informal written contexts, as in 'Who's going to the cinema?', 'Who's been eating garlic?' and 'Who's afraid of spiders'. **Whose** is a possessive pronoun or possessive adjective, as in 'That's the woman whose house was burgled', 'Whose hat is this?' and 'Whose are they?'.

-ways is prefix which to some extent acts an alternative to 'wise' in its first two meanings, as in crabways and lengthways.

-wise is a prefix with several meanings It can mean 'indicating manner or way', as in clockwise and crabwise. It can also mean' in the position or direction of' as in lengthwise and breadthwise. It can also mean 'with reference to', as in 'careerwise, familywise. jobwise and salarywise. This last use is very much over-used. -Wise can also mean 'clever, sensible', as in streetwise and worldlywise.

Z

zero plural refers to a plural form that has the same form as the singular. Examples include 'cod', 'deer', 'grouse' (gamebird) and 'sheep'. Some nouns have ordinary plurals and **zero plurals** as alternatives, as 'fish/fishes'. Nouns of measurement often have **zero plurals**, as in 'She is five foot three' and 'Six dozen eggs'.

zeugma is a figure of speech which uses a single word to apply to two words which are not appropriate to each other, as in 'We collected our coats and our baby', 'She left the building and her job', and 'She left in taxi and a fit of hysterics'. **Zeugma** is similar to BATHOS.

Appendix I

All of us have problem words that cause spelling difficulties but there are some words that are generally misspelt. These inlcude:

A
abbreviation
abscess
absence
abysmal
accelerator
accessible
accessories
accommodate
accompaniment
accumulate
accurate
accustomed
achieve
aching
acknowledge
acknowledgement/
  acknowledgment
acquaint
acquaintance
acquiesce
acquiescence
acquire
acquit
acquittal
acreage
across
actual
additional
address

adequate
adieu
adjacent
admissible
admittance
adolescence
adolescent
advantageous
advertisement
advice
advise
aerate
aerial
aesthetic
affect
affiliation
afforestation
aggravate
aggravation
aggregate
aggression
aggressive
aghast
agnosticism
agoraphobia
agreeable
agreed
aisle
alcohol
alfresco

alibis
align
alignment
allege
allergic
alleys
alligator
allocate
allotment
allotted
almond
alms
alphabetically
already
although
aluminium
ambiguous
amethyst
ammunition
anachronism
anaesthetic
analyse
analysis
anarchist
ancestor
ancestry
anemone
angrily
anguish
annihilate

annihilation
anniversary
announcement
annulled
annulment
anonymous
anorak
answered
Antarctic
antibiotic
antithesis
anxiety
apartheid
apologize
appalling
apparently
appearance
appendicitis
appreciate
approval
aquarium
aquiline
arbiter
arbitrary
arbitration
archaeology
architectural
Arctic
arguably
arrangement
arrival
artichoke
ascend
ascent
asphalt
asphyxiate
asphyxiation

assassin
assassinate
assessment
assistance
associate
asthma
asthmatic
astrakhan
atheist
atrocious
attach
attendant
attitude
aubergine
auburn
auctioneer
audible
aural
automatic
autumn
awful
awkward

B

bachelor
bagatelle
baggage
bailiff
ballast
ballerina
banana
banister
bankruptcy
banquet
barbecue
barometer
barrister

basically
basis
bassoon
battalion
bazaar
beautiful
befriend
beguile
behaviour
beleaguer
belief
believe
belligerent
benefited
bequeath
berserk
besiege
bettered
bevelled
bewitch
bias
bicycle
biennial
bigamous
bigoted
bilingual
biscuit
bivouacked
blancmange
blasphemous
blasphemy
bleary
blitz
bodily
bonfire
bootee
borough

bouquet

bourgeois

boutique

bracketed

braille

brassiere

breadth

breathalyser

brief

broccoli

brochure

bronchitis

bruise

brusque

buccaneer

Buddhist

budding

budgerigar

budgeted

buffeted

bulletin

bumptious

bungalow

buoyancy

buoyant

bureau

bureaucracy

business

buttoned

C

cabbage

cafeteria

caffeine

camouflage

campaign

campaigned

cancelled

cancerous

candour

cannabis

cannibal

canvassing

capability

capillary

capitalist

caravan

carbohydrate

carburettor

career

caress

caries

carriage

cartoonist

cashier

cassette

castanets

casualty

catalogue

catarrh

catechism

catering

cauliflower

cautious

ceiling

cellophane

cemetery

centenary

centilitre

centimetre

certainty

champagne

championed

chancellor

changeable

channelled

characteristic

chasm

chauffeur

cheetah

cherish

chief

chilblain

chintz

chiropody

chisel

choreographer

choreography

chronically

chrysanthemum

cigarette

cinnamon

circuitous

cistern

civilian

claustrophobia

clientele

clique

coalesce

cocoa

coconut

coffee

cognac

coincidence

colander

collaborate

collapsible

colleague

colonel

colossal

comically

commandeer
commemorate
commentator
commercial
commiserate
commission
commissionaire
commitment
committal
committed
committee
communicate
commuter
companion
comparative
comparison
compatibility
compelled
competitive
computer
conceal
concealment
conceit
conceive
concession
concurrent
concussion
condemned
condescend
confectionery
conference
confetti
congeal
congratulations
conjunctivitis
conned
connoisseur

conscience
conscientious
conscious
consequently
consignment
consolation
conspicuous
constitute
consumer
contemptible
continent
continuous
contraception
contradictory
controlled
controller
controversial
convalesce
convenient
convertible
conveyed
convolvulus
coolly
cooperate
cooperative
coordinate
copying
coquette
corduroy
co-respondent
coronary
correspondence
correspondent
corridor
corroborate
corrugated
cosmopolitan

cosseted
councillor
counselling
counterfeit
courageous
courteous
crèche
credible
credited
crematorium
creosote
crescent
crisis
criterion
crocheted
crocodile
croupier
crucial
crucifixion
cruelly
cruise
cryptic
cubicle
cupful
curable
curiosity
curious
currency
curriculum vitae
customary
cynic
cynicism
cynosure

D

dachshund
daffodil

dahlia
dais
damage
dandruff
darkened
debatable
debauched
debility
deceased
deceit
deceive
deciduous
decipher
decoyed
decrease
decreed
defamatory
defeat
defendant
defied
definite
definitely
dehydrate
deign
deliberate
delicatessen
delicious
delinquent
delirious
demeanour
demonstrate
denouement
denunciation
dependence
depth
derailment
dermatitis

derogatory
descend
descendant
desiccate
desperate
detach
detachable
detergent
deterred
deterrent
deuce
develop
developed
development
diabetes
diagnosis
dialogue
diametrically
diaphragm
diarrhoea
difference
different
dilapidated
dilemma
dilettante
diminish
diminution
dinosaur
diphtheria
diphthong
disadvantageous
disagreeable
disagreed
disagreement
disappearance
disappeared
disappoint

disapproval
disastrous
disbelief
disbelieve
discipline
discotheque
discouraging
discourteous
discrepancy
discrimination
discussion
disease
disguise
dishevelled
dishonourable
disillusion
disinfectant
disinherited
dismissal
disobeyed
disparage
dispelled
disposal
dispossess
dissatisfaction
dissatisfy
dissect
disseminate
dissent
dissimilar
dissipated
dissipation
dissociate
dissolute
dissuade
distilled
distillery

distinguish
distraught
disuse
divisible
documentary
doggerel
domineering
donate
doubt
dragooned
drastically
draughty
drooled
drooped
drunkenness
dubious
dumbfounded
dungarees
duress
dutiful
dynamite
dysentery
dyspepsia

E
eccentric
ecclesiastic
ecologically
economically
ecstasy
eczema
effective
effervescence
efficacious
efficient
effrontery
eightieth

elaborate
electrician
elevenses
eligible
emancipate
embarrass
embarrassment
emergence
emergent
emolument
emotional
emphasize
employee
emptied
enable
encourage
encyclopedia
endeavour
endurance
energetically
enervate
engineer
enough
ensuing
entailed
enthusiasm
enumerate
epilepsy
equalize
equalled
equipped
erroneous
erudite
escalator
escapism
espionage
essence

essential
estranged
etiquette
euthanasia
eventually
evidently
exaggerate
exaggeration
exalt
exasperate
exceed
exceedingly
excellent
excessive
exchequer
excommunicate
exercise
exhaust
exhibit
exhilarate
exorcise
explanation
exquisite
extinguish
extraneous
extravagant

F
fabulous
facetious
faeces
Fahrenheit
fallacious
fanatic
farcical
fascinate
fatigue

fatuous	freight	global
February	frequency	gluttonous
feeler	friend	glycerine
feign	frolicked	gnarled
ferocious	fuchsia	gnash
festooned	fugitive	goitre
feud	fulfil	gossiped
feudal	fulfilled	government
fevered	fulfilment	graffiti
fiasco	fullness	grammar
fibre	fulsome	grandeur
fictitious	furious	gratefully
fiend	furniture	gratitude
fierce	furthered	gratuitous
fiery		greetings
filial	**G**	gregarious
finesse	gaiety	grief
flabbergasted	galloped	grieve
flaccid	garrison	grovelled
flammable	garrotted	gruesome
flannelette	gases	guarantee
fluent	gateau	guarantor
fluoridate	gauge	guard
fluoride	gazetteer	guardian
fluoridize	geisha	guest
foliage	generator	guillotine
forcible	genuine	guinea
foreignor	gerbil	guise
forfeit	gesticulate	guitar
forthwith	ghastly	gymkhana
fortieth	ghetto	gypsy/gipsy
fortuitous	gigantic	
fortunately	gingham	**H**
frailty	giraffe	haemoglobin
frankincense	glamorous	haemorrhage
fraudulent	glamour	halcyon
freedom	glimpse	hallucination

225

hammered
handfuls
handicapped
handkerchief
happened
harangue
harass
harlequin
haughty
hazard
hearse
height
heightened
heinous
heir
herbaceous
hereditary
heroism
hesitate
hiccup, hiccough
hideous
hierarchy
hieroglyphics
hijack
hilarious
hindrance
hippopotamus
holiday
holocaust
homonym
honorary
honour
hooligan
horoscope
horrible
horticulture
hullabaloo

humorous
humour
hurricane
hurried
hygiene
hyphen
hypnosis
hypochondria
hypocrisy
hypotenuse
hypothesis
hypothetical
hysterical

I

icicle
ideological
idiosyncrasy
ignorance
illegible
illegitimate
illiberal
illiterate
imaginative
imitation
immaculate
immediate
immemorial
immoral
immovable
impasse
impeccable
imperative
imperceptible
imperious
impetuous
implacable

impresario
imprisoned
imprisonment
inaccessible
inadmissible
inappropriate
inaugural
incandescent
incessant
incipient
incognito
incommunicado
inconceivable
incongruous
incontrovertible
incorrigible
incredulous
incriminate
incubator
incurred
indefatigable
indefinable
indefinite
independence
independent
indescribable
indict
indictment
indigenous
indigestible
indomitable
indubitable
ineligible
inescapable
inexcusable
inexhaustible
infallible

infatuated
inferred
infinitive
inflamed
inflammable
inflationary
ingratiate
ingredient
inhabitant
inheritance
inhibition
iniquitous
initiate
initiative
innate
innocuous
innumerable
innumerate
inoculate
insecticide
inseparable
insincere
insistence
instalment
instantaneous
intercept
interference
interior
intermediate
intermittent
interpret
interpretation
interrogate
interrupt
interview
intrigue
intrinsically

intuition
intuitive
invariably
inveigle
inveterate
involuntary
involvement
irascible
irrelevant
irreparable
irreplaceable
irresistible
irresponsible
irrevocable
irritable
italicize
itinerant
itinerary

J

jackal
jeopardize
jettisoned
jewellery
jodhpurs
juggernaut
jugular

K

kaleidoscopic
karate
keenness
khaki
kidnapped
kilometre
kiosk
kitchenette

kleptomania
knick-knack
knowledgeable
kowtow

L

labelled
laboratory
labyrinth
lackadaisical
laddered
lager
language
languor
languorous
laryngitis
larynx
lassitude
latitude
laundered
launderette
layette
league
leanness
ledger
legendary
legible
legitimate
length
lengthened
leukaemia
levelled
liaise
liaison
lieu
lieutenant
lilac

227

limousine
lineage
linen
lingerie
linguist
liqueur
literature
litre
livelihood
loneliness
loosened
loquacious
lorgnette
lucrative
lucre
luggage
lugubrious
luminous
luscious
lustre
luxurious
lyric

M
macabre
maelstrom
magician
magnanimous
mahogany
maintenance
malaise
malaria
malignant
manageable
management
mannequin
manoeuvre

mantelpiece
manually
margarine
marijuana
marquee
martyr
marvellous
marzipan
masochist
massacre
matinee
mayonnaise
meagre
measurement
medallion
medieval
mediocre
melancholy
meningitis
meringue
messenger
meteorological
metropolitan
microphone
midday
migraine
mileage
milieu
millionaire
mimicked
mimicry
miniature
miraculous
mirrored
miscellaneous
mischief
mischievous

misogynist
misshapen
misspell
misspent
modelled
modelling
morgue
mortgage
mosquito
mountaineer
moustache
multitudinous
muscle
museum
mysterious
mythical

N
naive
narrative
naughty
nausea
nautical
necessary
necessity
negligence
negligible
negotiate
neighbourhood
neither
neurotic
neutral
niche
niece
ninetieth
ninth
nocturnal

nonentity
notably
noticeably
notoriety
nuance
numbered
numerate
numerous
nutrient
nutritious

O
obedient
obese
obituary
oblige
oblique
oblivious
obnoxious
obscene
obscenity
obsessive
obstetrician
occasion
occupancy
occupier
occupying
occurred
occurrence
octogenarian
odorous
odour
offence
offered
official
officious
ominous

omission
omitted
oneself
opaque
ophthalmic
opinion
opponent
opportunity
opposite
orchestra
ordinary
original
orthodox
orthopaedic
oscillate
ostracize
outlying
outrageous
overdraft
overrate
overreach
overwrought
oxygen

P
pacifist
pageant
pamphlet
panacea
panegyric
panicked
papered
parachute
paraffin
paragraph
paralyse
paralysis

paraphernalia
parcelled
parliament
paroxysm
parquet
partially
participant
particle
partner
passenger
passers-by
pastime
patterned
pavilion
peaceable
peculiar
pejorative
pencilled
penicillin
peppered
perceive
perennial
perilous
permissible
permitted
pernicious
perpetrate
persistence
personnel
persuasion
perusal
pessimism
pessimistically
pesticide
phantom
pharmacy
pharyngitis

pharynx
phenomenon
phial
phlegm
physician
physiotherapist
picketed
picnic
picnicked
picturesque
pioneered
pious
piteous
pitiful
plaintiff
plausible
pleurisy
pneumonia
poignant
politician
pollution
polythene
porridge
portrait
portray
positive
possession
possibility
posthumous
potatoes
precede
precedent
precinct
precipice
precocious
preference
preferred

prejudice
preliminary
prepossessing
prerequisite
prerogative
prescription
presence
preservative
prestige
prestigious
pretentious
prevalent
priest
primitive
procedure
proceed
procession
professional
profiteering
prohibit
promiscuous
pronunciation
propeller
proposal
proprietor
prosecute
protagonist
protein
provocation
prowess
psalm
psyche
psychiatric
psychic
publicly
pursuit
putative

pyjamas

Q
quarrelsome
questionnaire
queue
quintet

R
rabies
radioed
radios
railing
rancour
ransack
rapturous
reassurance
rebelled
rebellious
recalcitrant
receipt
receive
recommend
reconnaissance
reconnoitre
recruitment
recurrence
redundant
referee
reference
referred
regatta
regrettable
regretted
rehabilitation
reign
relevant

relief
relieve
reminisce
reminiscence
remuneration
rendezvous
repertoire
repetitive
reprieve
reprisal
requisite
rescind
resemblance
reservoir
resistance
resourceful
responsibility
restaurant
restaurateur
resurrection
resuscitate
retrieve
reunion
reveille
revelry
revenue
reversible
rhapsody
rheumatism
rhododendron
rhomboid
rhubarb
rhyme
rhythm
ricochet
righteous
rigorous

rigour
risotto
riveted
rogue
roughage
roulette
royalty
rucksack
ruinous
rummage
rumour

S

sabotage
sacrilege
saddened
salmon
salvage
sanctuary
sandwich
sanitary
sapphire
satellite
scaffolding
scandalous
scenic
sceptre
schedule
scheme
schizophrenic
schooner
sciatica
science
scissors
scruple
scrupulous
scurrilous

scythe
secretarial
secretary
sedative
sedentary
sensitive
separate
sergeant
serrated
serviceable
serviette
settee
shampooed
shattered
sheikh
sheriff
shield
shovelled
shuddered
siege
significant
silhouette
simply
simultaneous
sincerely
sixtieth
skeleton
skilful
slanderous
slaughter
sleigh
sleight of hand
sluice
smattering
smithereens
snivelled
soccer

solemn	successful	tangerine
solicitor	successor	tangible
soliloquy	succinct	tattoo
soloist	succulent	technique
sombre	succumb	teenager
somersault	suddenness	televise
sophisticated	suede	temperature
sovereign	sufficient	tenuous
spaghetti	suffocate	terrifically
spectre	suicide	terrifying
spherical	sullenness	territory
sphinx	summoned	terrorist
sponsor	supercilious	therapeutic
spontaneity	superfluous	therefore
spontaneous	supersede	thief
squabble	supervise	thinness
squandered	supervisor	thirtieth
squawk	supplementary	thorough
staccato	surgeon	thoroughfare
staggered	surveillance	threshold
stammered	surveyor	thrombosis
statistics	susceptible	throughout
statutory	suspicious	thwart
stealth	sweetener	thyme
stereophonic	sycamore	tightened
stirrup	symmetry	titivate
storage	sympathize	tobacconist
strait-laced	symphony	toboggan
straitjacket	synagogue	toffee
strategic	syndicate	tomatoes
strength	synonym	tomorrow
strenuous	syringe	tonsillitis
stupor		topsy turvy
suave	**T**	tornadoes
subpoena		torpedoes
subtle	tableau	torpor
succeed	taciturn	tortoiseshell
	taffeta	

tortuous
totalled
tourniquet
towelling
trafficked
tragedy
traitorous
tranquillity
tranquillizer
transcend
transferable
transferred
transparent
travelled
traveller
tremor
troublesome
trousseau
truism
trustee
tsetse
tuberculosis
tumour
tunnelled
tureen
turquoise
twelfth
typhoon
tyranny

U
unanimous
unconscious
undoubted
unduly
unequalled
unique

unnecessary
unremitting
unrequited
unrivalled
upheaval
uproarious

V
vaccinate
vacuum
vague
vanilla
variegate
vehement
vendetta
veneer
ventilator
verandah
vermilion
veterinary
vetoes
vice versa
vicissitude
vicissitudes
vigorous
vigour
viscount
visibility
vivacious
vociferous
voluminous
volunteered
vulnerable

W
walkie-talkie
walloped

warrior
wastage
watered
weakened
wearisome
Wednesday
weight
weird
whereabouts
wherewithal
widened
width
wield
wintry
witticism
wizened
woebegone
wooden
woollen
worsened
worship
worshipped
wrapper
wrath
wreak
writhe

X
xylophone

Y
yield
yoghurt

Z
zealous
zigzagged

233

Appendix II

Some words with totally different meanings have similar spellings and therefore can be easily confused. Some examples are:

aboard	affect	allusion	angel
abroad	effect	delusion	angle
		illusion	
accept	affluent		annals
except	effluent	altar	annuals
		alter	
access	ail		annex
excess	ale	alteration	annexe
		altercation	
acme	air		annuals
acne	heir	alternately	annals
		alternatively	
ad	all		antiquated
add	awl	amateur	antique
		amateurish	
adapter	allay		arc
adaptor	alley	amend	ark
		emend	
addition	allegory		arisen
edition	allergy	amiable	arose
		amicable	
adverse	alley		artist
averse	allay	among	artiste
		between	
advice	alliterate		ascent
advise	illiterate	amoral	assent
		immoral	
aesthetic	allude	immortal	ascetic
ascetic	elude		aesthetic

235

assay	ball	bean	belief
essay	bawl	been	believe
		being	
assent	ballet		bell
ascent	ballot	beat	belle
		beet	
astrology	banns		bellow
astronomy	bans	beau	below
		bow	
ate	bare		beret
eaten	bear	became	berry
		become	bury
aural	barn		
oral	baron	beech	berth
	barren	beach	birth
averse			
adverse	base	been	beside
	bass	bean	besides
awl		being	
all	bated		between
	baited	beer	among
axes		bier	
axis	bath		bid
	bathe	beet	bade
bad		beat	
bade	baton		bier
	batten	befallen	beer
bade		befell	
bid	bawl		bight
	ball	began	bite
bail		begun	
bale	bazaar		birth
bale out	bizarre	being	berth
		bean	
baited	beach	been	bit
bated	beech		bitten

236

bite	bookie	bow	breech
bight	bouquet	bough	breach
bizarre	boor	boy	bridal
bazaar	boar	buoy	bridle
	bore		
blew		brae	broach
blown	boost	bray	brooch
	boast		
blew		brake	broke
blue	bootee	break	broken
	booty		
bloc		brassière	brooch
block	bore	brazier	broach
	boar		
blond	boor	bray	buffet
blonde		brae	[buffit]
	bore		buffet
blown	born	brazier	[boofa]
blew	borne	brassière	
			buoy
blue	borough	breach	boy
blew	burgh	breech	
			burgh
boar	bough	bread	borough
boor	bow	bred	
bore			bury
	bound	break	berry
board	bounded	brake	
bored			
	bouquet	breath	but
boast	bookie	breathe	butt
boost			
	blow	bred	buy
bonny	beau	bread	by
bony			bye

237

cache	cartilage	cereal	chord
cash	cartridge	serial	cord
caddie	carton	chafe	chose
caddy	cartoon	chaff	choose
			chosen
calf	cartridge	charted	
calve	cartilage	chartered	chute
			shoot
callous	cash	chased	
callus	cache	chaste	cite
			sight
calve	cast	cheap	site
calf	caste	cheep	
			clothes
came	cavalier	check	cloths
come	cavalry	cheque	
			coarse
canned	ceiling	checked	course
could	sealing	chequered	
			collage
cannon	cell	cheep	college
canon	sell	cheap	
			coma
can't	cellular	cheque	comma
cant	cellulose	check	
			come
canvas	censor	chilli	came
canvass	censure	chilly	
			comma
carat	cent	choir	coma
carrot	scent	quire	
	sent		commissionaire
cart		choose	commissioner
kart	centenarian	chose	
	centenary	chosen	complement
			compliment

complemen-
tary

complimen-
tary

concert
consort

confidant
confidante
confident

conscience
conscientious
conscious

consort
concert

consul
council
counsel

continual
continuous

coop
coup

coral
corral

cord
chord

co-respondent
correspondent

cornet
coronet

cornflour
cornflower

coronet
cornet

corps
corpse

corral
coral

correspondent
co-respondent

cost
costed

could
canned

council
counsel
consul

councillor
counsellor

coup
coop

course
coarse

courtesy
curtsy

creak
creek

crevasse
crevice

crochet
crotchet

cue
queue

curb
kerb

currant
current

curtsy
courtesy

cygnet
signet

cymbal
symbol

diary
diary

dam
damn

dammed
damned

damn
dam

dear
deer

decry
descry

deer
dear

delusion
allusion
illusion

dependant
dependent

deprecate
depreciate

descendant
descendent

descry
decry

desert
dessert

device
devise

devolution	dough	due	economic
evolution	doe	dew	economical
		Jew	
dew	draft		edition
due	draught	duel	addition
Jew		dual	
	dragon		eerie
diary	dragoon	dully	eyrie
dairy		duly	
	draught		effect
did	draft	dungeon	affect
done		dudgeon	
	drawn		effluent
die	drew	dux	affluent
dye		ducks	
	drank		elder
died	drunk	dye	eldest
dyed		die	
	drew		elicit
dinghy	drawn	dyed	illicit
dingy		died	
	driven		eligible
disbelief	drove	dyeing	legible
disbelieve		dying	
	drunk		ellipse
discus	drank	earthly	eclipse
discuss		earthy	
	dual		elude
doe	duel	easterly	allude
dough		eastern	
	ducks		emend
doily	dux	eaten	amend
dolly		ate	
	dudgeon	eclipse	emigrant
done	dungeon	ellipse	immigrant
did			

emigration	escapement	expend	fate
immigration	escarpment	expand	fête
emission	essay	expensive	faun
omission	assay	expansive	fawn
emphasis	etymologist	expiate	feat
emphasize	entomologist	expatiate	feet
employee	evolution	extant	feign
employer	devolution	extinct	fain
ensure	ewe	eyrie	feint
insure	yew	eerie	faint
	you		
entomologist		faerie	fell
etymologist	except	fairy	fallen
	accept		felled
envelop		fain	
envelope	excess	feign	ferment
	access		foment
epigram		faint	
epitaph	executioner	feint	fête
epithet	executor		fate
		fair	
ere	exercise	fare	fiancé
err	exorcise		fiancée
		fairy	
erotic	expand	faerie	filed
erratic	expend		filled
		fallen	
err	expansive	fell	final
ere	expensive	felled	finale
erratic	expatiate	fare	fir
erotic	expiate	fair	fur

fission
fissure

flair
flare

flammable
inflammable

flare
flair

flea
flee

flew
flu
flue

flew
flown

flocks
phlox

floe
flow

flour
flower

floury
flowery

flow
flow

flower
flour

flowery
floury

flown
flew

flue
flue
flew

foment
ferment

font
fount

forbade
forbidden

fore
four

foregone
forgone

foresaw
foreseen

foreword
forward

forgave
forgiven

forgone
foregone

forgone
forwent

forgot
forgotten

forsaken
forsook

forswore
forsworn

fort
forte
forty

forth
fourth

forty
fort
forte

forward
foreword

forwent
forgone

foul
fowl

found
founded

fount
font

four
fore

fourth
forth

fowl
foul

franc
frank

freeze
frieze

froze
frozen

funeral
funereal

fur
fir

gabble
gable

gaff
gaffe

gait
gate

galleon glacier grope hanged
gallon glazier group hung

gamble goal ground hanger
gambol gaol grounded hangar

gaol gone grown hare
goal went grew hair

gate gorilla guerrilla hart
gait guerrilla gorilla heart

gave gourmand guild heal
given gourmet gild heel

genie gradation guilt hoar
genius graduation gilt here
genus
grate hail heart
genteel great hale hart
gentile
gentle grew hair heel
grown hare heal
genus
genie grief half heir
genius grieve halve air

gild gilll hallo hore
guild grille hallow hear
halo
gilt griped heron
guilt gripped halve herring
half
given grisly hew
gave gristly hangar hue
grizzly hanger

hewed	horde	immigrant	inflammable
hewn	hoard	emigrant	flammable
hid	horse	immigration	ingenious
hidden	hoarse	emigration	ingenuous
higher	hue	immoral	inhuman
hire	hew	amoral	inhumane
		immortal	
him	human		insure
hymn	humane	immorality	ensure
		immortality	
hire	humiliation		intelligent
higher	humility	impetuous	intelligible
		impetus	
hoar	hung		interment
whore	hanged	impracticable	internment
		impractical	
hoard	hymn		invertebrate
horde	him	inapt	inveterate
		inept	
hoarse	idle		jam
horse	idol		jamb
		incredible	
hole	illegible	incredulous	Jew
whole	ineligible		dew
		indigenous	due
honorary	illicit	indigent	
honourable	elicit		jib
		industrial	jibe
hoop	illiterate	industrious	
whoop	alliterate		judicial
		ineligible	judicious
hoped	illusion	illegible	
hopped	allusion		junction
	delusion	inept	juncture
		inapt	

kart	know	layer	liar
cart	no	lair	lyre
kerb	known	lea	libel
curb	knew	lee	liable
key	lade	lead	licence
quay	laid	led	license
	lay		
knave	lied	leak	lied
nave		leek	lade
	lain		laid
knead	lane	led	lay
kneed		lead	
need	lair		lightening
	layer	lee	lightning
knew		lea	
known	lama		lineament
	llama	leek	liniment
knew		leak	
new	lane		liqueur
	lain	legible	liquor
knight		eligible	
night	laterally		literal
	latterly	lemming	literary
knightly		lemon	literate
nightly	lath		
	lathe	leopard	llama
knit		leper	lama
nit	latterly		
	laterally	lessen	load
knot		lesson	lode
not	lay		
	lade	liable	loan
knotty	laid	libel	lone
naughty	lied		

245

loath	lyre	mare	medal
loathe	liar	mayor	meddle
local	macaroni	marina	mediate
locale	macaroon	merino	meditate
lode	made	marshal	meet
load	maid	martial	meat
			mete out
lone	magnate	marten	
loan	magnet	martin	merino
			marina
looped	maid	martial	
loped	made	marshal	metal
lopped			mettle
	mail	martin	
loose	male	marten	mete out
lose			meat
	main	mask	meet
loot	mane	masque	
lute			meter
	maize	mat	metre
loped	maze	matt	
lopped			mettle
looped	male	mayor	metal
	mail	mare	
lose			mews
loose	mane	maze	muse
	main	maize	
loth			mien
loathe	maniac	mean	mean
	manic	mien	
lumbar			might
lumber	manner	meat	mite
	manor	meet	
lute		mete out	miner
loot			minor

minister	mote	nave	nit
minster	moat	knave	knit
missal	motif	navel	no
missile	motive	naval	know
mistaken	mouse	navvy	northerly
mistook	moose	navy	northern
	mousse		
mite		nay	not
might	mucous	née	knot
	mucus	neigh	
moat			nougat
mote	multiple	need	nugget
	multiply	knead	
modal		kneed	nought
model	muscle		naught
module	mussel	negligent	
		negligible	nugget
momentary	muse		nougat
momentous	mews	neigh	
momentum		nay	oar
	mussel	née	ore
moose	muscle		
mouse		net	of
mousse	mystic	nett	off
	mystique		
moped		new	official
mopped	naught	knew	officious
	nought		
moral		night	omission
morale	naughty	knight	omission
	knotty		
morality		nightly	oral
mortality	naval	knightly	aural
	navel		

ore	palate	peak	pennies
oar	palette	peek	pence
	pallet	pique	
organism			perquisite
orgasm	pale	peal	prerequisite
	pail	peel	
outdid			personal
outdone	palette	pear	personnel
	palate	pair	
overcame	pallet	pare	petrel
overcome			petrol
	pane	pearl	
overdid	pain	purl	pheasant
overdone			peasant
	par	peasant	
overran	parr	pheasant	phlox
overrun			flocks
	pare	pedal	
overtaken	pear	peddle	piazza
overtook	pair		pizza
		peek	
overthrew	parr	peak	piece
overthrown	par	pique	peace
packed	passed	peel	pier
pact	past	peal	peer
pail	pastel	peer	pined
pale	pastille	pier	pinned
pain	pate	pence	piped
pane	pâté	pennies	pipped
	patty		
pair		pendant	pique
pare	peace	pendent	peak
pear	piece		peek

pistil	pore	price	prophet
pistol	pour	prise	profit
		prize	
pizza	pored		propriety
piazza	poured	principal	property
		principle	
place	poser		prostate
plaice	poseur	prise	prostate
		price	
plain	pour	prize	prove
plane	pore		proof
		private	
plaintiff	poured	privet	pull
plaintive	pored		pool
		prize	
plait	practicable	prise	purl
plate	practical	price	pearl
plane	practice	proceed	put
plain	practise	precede	putt
plate	pray	profit	quash
plait	prey	prophet	squash
plum	precede	program	quay
plumb	proceed	programme	key
politic	premier	proof	queue
political	première	prove	cue
pool	prerequisite	property	quiet
pull	perquisite	propricty	quite
poplar	prey	prophecy	quire
popular	pray	prophesy	choir

quite	rapped	reproof	rite
quiet	rapt	reprove	right
	wrapped		write
racket		respectful	
racquet	rated	respective	road
	ratted		rode
radar		rest	rowed
raider	raze	wrest	
	raise		rode
raged		retch	ridden
ragged	read	wretch	
	red		roe
raider		review	row
radar	read	revue	
	reed		rôle
rain		rhyme	roll
reign	real	rime	
rein	reel		rose
		ridden	risen
raise	red	rode	
raze	read		rote
		right	wrote
rampant	reel	rite	
rampart	real	write	rough
			ruff
ran	refuge	rime	
run	refugee	rhyme	rout
			route
rang	regal	ring	
ringed	regale	wring	row
rung			roe
	reign	ringed	
rap	rain	rang	rowed
wrap	rein	rung	road
			rode
raped	relief	risen	
rapped	relieve	rose	

ruff	scene	seen	sewed
rough	seen	saw	sewn
run	scent	seen	sewer
ran	cent	scene	sower
	sent		
rung		seer	sewn
wrung	sceptic	sear	sewed
	septic	sere	
rye			sewn
wry	scraped	sell	sown
	scrapped	cell	
sail			sextant
sale	sculptor	sensual	sexton
	sculpture	sensuous	
salon			shaken
saloon	sea	sent	shook
	see	scent	
sang		scent	shear
sung	sealing		sheer
	ceiling	septic	
sank		sceptic	sheared
sunk	seam		sheered
sunken	seem	sere	shorn
		sear	
saviour	sear	seer	shelf
savour	seer		shelve
	sere	serial	
saw		cereal	shoe
seen	secret		shoo
	secrete	series	
sawed		serious	shook
sawn	see		shaken
	sea	sew	
scared		so	shoot
scarred	seem	sow	chute
	seam		

shorn	slated	sole	speciality
sheared	slatted	soul	specialty
sheered			
	slay	some	species
showed	sleigh	sum	specious
shown			
	slew	son	sped
shrank	slain	sun	speeded
shrunk			
	sloe	soot	spoke
sight	slow	suit	spoken
cite			
site	sloped	sore	sprang
	slopped	soar	sprung
signet			
cygnet	slow	soul	squash
	sloe	sole	quash
silicon			
silicone	smelled	southerly	staid
	smelt	southern	stayed
singeing			
singing	sniped	sow	stair
	snipped	sew	stare
sinuous		so	
sinus	so		stake
	sew	sowed	steak
site	sow	sown	
cite			stalk
sight	soar	sower	stock
	sore	sewer	
skies			stanch
skis	sociable	sown	staunch
	social	sewn	
slain			stank
slew	solder	spared	stunk
	soldier	sparred	

stare	stocked	style	swam
stair	stoked	stile	swum
stared	storey	suede	swede
starred	story	swede	suede
stationary	straight	suit	sweet
stationery	strait	soot	suite
statue	straightened	suite	swelled
statute	straitened	sweet	swollen
staunch	stratum	sum	swingeing
stanch	stratus	some	swinging
stayed	strewed	summary	swollen
staid	strewn	summery	swelled
steak	strife	sun	swore
stake	strive	son	sworn
steal	striped	sundae	swum
steel	stripped	Sunday	swam
step	strive	sung	symbol
steppe	strife	sang	cymbal
stile	striven	sunk	tacks
style	strove	sank	tax
		sunken	
stimulant	stunk		tail
stimulus	stank	super	tale
		supper	
stock	sty		taken
stalk	stye	surplice	took
		surplus	

tale	teem	throne	to
tail	team	thrown	too
			two
taped	teeth	through	
tapped	teethe	thorough	toe
			tow
taper	temporal	through	
tapir	temporary	threw	tomb
			tome
tapped	tendon	thrown	
taped	tenon	throne	ton
			tonne
tare	tenor	throws	tun
tear	tenure	throes	
			too
taught	testimonial	thyme	to
taut	testimony	time	two
tax	their	tic	took
tacks	there	tick	taken
	they're		
tea		tier	topi
tee	thorough	tear	toupee
	through		
team		tiled	tore
teem	thrash	tilled	torn
	thresh		
tear		timber	tow
tare	threw	timbre	toe
	through		
tear		time	trait
tier	threw	thyme	tray
	thrown		
tee		tire	treaties
tea	throes	tyre	treatise
	throws		

254

trod	urban	waged	weekly
trodden	urbane	wagged	weakly
troop	vacation	waif	weigh
troupe	vocation	waive	way
		wave	
tun	vain		went
ton	vane	waist	gone
tonne	vein	waste	
			westerly
turban	vale	want	western
turbine	veil	wont	
			wet
two	venal	warden	whet
to	venial	warder	
too			whit
	veracity	ware	wit
tycoon	voracity	wear	
typhoon			whole
	vertex	waste	hole
tyre	vortex	waist	
tire			whoop
	vigilant	wave	hoop
unaware	vigilante	waif	
unawares		waive	whore
	vocation		hoar
unconscion-	vacation	waver	
able		wafer	willed
unconscious	voracity		would
	veracity	way	
undid		weigh	winded
undone	vortex		wound
	vertex	weak	
unwanted		week	wit
unwonted	wafer		whit
	waver	wear	
		ware	

withdrawn	would	wreath	wrote
withdrew	willed	wreathe	written
wittily	would	wrest	wrung
wittingly	wood	rest	rung
	wooed		
woe		wretch	wry
woo	wove	retch	rye
	woven		
woke		wring	yew
woken	wrap	ring	ewe
	rap		you
wont		write	
want		right	yoke
	wrapped	rite	yolk
woo	rapped		
woe	rapt	wrote	yore
		rote	your
wore	wreak		
worn	wreck		